DISTILLING SCOTLAND

ROCA LLIBRES

DISTILLING SCOTLAND

JOAN, JOSEP & JORDI ROCA

ROCA LLIBRES

Scott McCroskie, Managing Director of The Macallan

FOREWORD

It has been an honour for the team at The Macallan to collaborate with the remarkable founders of El Celler de Can Roca – Joan, Josep and Jordi Roca. We have developed an extraordinary partnership together.

As The Macallan embarks on a new chapter of its story with the opening of our groundbreaking new distillery and visitor experience, it is apt to reflect upon and celebrate the journey we have taken with our friends.

Over the past five years, we have explored innovation, creativity and collaboration with the Rocas – undoubtedly among the world's most visionary and accomplished masters of cuisine. By exploring each other's fascinating worlds, we have discovered much in common. This in turn has led to the creation of a true collaboration built on shared values and beliefs. From a commitment to the seeking perfection in everything we do, our passion for our product, and a belief in embracing and working with time to ensure the best outcomes, our aligned perspective has provided the basis for something really special and meaningful to everyone involved.

The Rocas enlightening tour of Scotland is an exploration of Scotland's land of exceptional food and drink, culminating in their arrival at the home of The Macallan in Speyside. Here they witnessed first-hand how our stunning landscape offers up some of the finest raw materials and ingredients which make our definitive single malt Scotch whisky.

With this book Joan, Josep and Jordi have not only successfully distilled Scotland, they have perfectly captured and reflected the power of our remarkable bond. We thank them for their ongoing passion for The Macallan and the endless energy they have invested in our partnership.

Scott McCroskie

Easter Elchies House at The Macallan Distillery

Isaac McHale, chef of The Clove Club restaurant

FOREWORD

The Roca brothers are writing a book about Scotland? Scotland? Really? I was surprised to get this message from Joan, asking me to write a foreword for their book celebrating my country. Would I take part? Of course!

El Celler de Can Roca. That name has always been synonymous with gastronomy for me. As a kid I used to go on holidays to St. Martí d'Empúries, near L'Escala, on the Spanish Costa Brava, and we used to fly into Girona, so I have always felt an affinity with the town and the region. We returned years later, and I went to my first 2-star restaurant in 2002, the old location. It was thrilling. To return years later, on my honeymoon last year, finally making it to the new location, was amazing. The restaurant has passed through several grand phases in gastronomy, 'looking to France and the haut bourgeois', 'Techno-emotional or Molecular', 'Sous-Vide' (but this probably falls in to the category before it) 'new naturalism/Nordic' and 'product-focused'. I lay these out because the last meal I had in Can Roca, in November last year, had so many highlights that looking back on the menu as a whole was to grasp how good it was. It was an Adventurous, Auteur cuisine. It was one which transmogrified ingredients in some dishes while letting them speak for themselves in others, one which showed their mastery of sous-vide cookery, without it becoming the reason for cooking a dish. It was one with stories, a menu that showed the excitement of travel and influences from around the world, while proudly remaining Catalan and Spanish, and using rare, local products, and making them the stars. We had Caesar's mushrooms, baby eels, mackerel with a tempeh made from fermented local Ganxet beans, langoustine with artemisia, squid with their innards, baby mullets and their livers, sardines steamed in sherry with a soup made from their bones, an amazing distillation of oyster shells and Chablis, suckling lamb tripe and brains, and hare with mole sauce, thickened with hare blood. I'm getting excited just thinking about it.

And so to the book. What would they be able to say, as outsiders, on the foods and traditions of my country? I have read the book now and I love it. It feels alive and current, while looking at the past and the traditions of food in Scotland. It asks interesting questions and explores how, as a country with some of the finest produce in the world, we didn't appreciate what we had and most of it was sold and shipped off to foreign lands where they valued the shellfish and mushrooms and wild game of our larder and would pay for them. As a country with a large part of its population living in urban areas, and a country that, at least in my experience, doesn't have as close a connection to its culinary heritage and stories, of which there are many, as other countries and cultures do, I hope that people read this book and learn about Scotland and its foods, the climate and geography that shaped them, and go and visit.

As described in the book, rapid urbanisation and industrialisation in the 18th century tore people from their communities and the areas they lived in, away from their local foods and customs, and as a result, much of these have been lost. This, coupled with the self-deprecating nature of the Scottish national identity, meant that we didn't value our food culture as other countries did, talked it down and felt that other countries' cuisines were inherently better. The fact of early industrialisation and the affects it had on population movement are, in my view, still felt today in the world's view of Scottish and British cuisine, with the bad reputation it has had for the past fifty years. Things have changed and moved on, and there is exciting cooking, delicious cooking and produce-focused cooking happening in Scotland right now, and we should be shouting about it from the rooftops. Restaurants like Inver, Timberyard, the Kitchin, The Cellar and Andrew Fairlie are amongst the best in the world. I hope that this book inspires people to learn more about the history of our beautiful country, a country of unicorns and castles, and witches and magic. And amazing food! Scotland I love you.

Bravo Joan, Josep and Jordi for writing this book and allowing me to see the beauty of my country through the eyes of an outsider, someone experiencing it for the first time. That is such an unexpected and wonderful viewpoint to be able to approach your own country from. Thank you all.

Isaac McHale

Yellowcraigs Beach

INTRODUCTION

At first, Scotland and cuisine don't seem to make the most renowned of pairs. So, what was it that made Joan, Josep and Jordi Roca set off on a culinary journey through Scotland? Curiosity! According to Samuel Johnson's *A Dictionary of the English Language*, first published in 1755, 'To travel is to make journeys of curiosity.'[1] The English lexicographer and writer, seeking an objective meaning of the verb 'to travel', used the word 'curiosity'; and thereby made way for this connotation: as the engine of a journey, curiosity has an expressive meaning.

This trip around Scotland isn't the first journey to be born from the insatiable culinary curiosity of the Roca brothers and turned into a book. However, it's not like any of their other accounts of culinary journeys. It is unique for various reasons, the most obvious being the location of Scotland: a country that is closer to Girona geographically than any of their other destinations, but also culturally exotic when viewed from a Mediterranean perspective. Another difference is the time that has been devoted to the journey: in the space of a year, the Roca brothers have spent almost one month travelling through this country that is approximately the same size as Andalusia. It is true, however, that this area includes 790 islands and almost twelve thousand kilometres — mainland Spain has less than four thousand — of zigzagging coastline, constantly interrupted by fjords and estuaries. But perhaps the greatest difference when compared to other journeys they've made is that this trip was inspired by and based on two travel journals from the eighteenth century: *A Journey to the Western Islands of Scotland*, by Samuel Johnson; and *The Journal of a Tour to the Hebrides*, by James Boswell.

---

1 Johnson, S. (1755). *A Dictionary of the English Language*. London: J. & P. Knapton.

FOLLOWING EIGHTEENTH-CENTURY MAPS

Samuel Johnson and James Boswell's paths crossed in London ten years before making their trip and they became firm friends. At the time, Dr Johnson was already a prominent figure and a learned man, in every sense of the word. What grew between them was almost a father-son relationship. The appearance of the Scotsman in Johnson's life is probably what awoke his interest in visiting Scotland, a country that he already viewed with a set of prejudices. The trip kept being postponed and Boswell's impatience to show his country to his English friend grew. In order to convince him, James Boswell got in touch with some of Johnson's other friends who were living in Scotland, asking them to invite him to stay. Eventually, towards the end of summer 1773, Johnson arrived in Edinburgh to start the trip. He was 63 years old and sure that he'd probably arrived too late to witness the wild Scotland that he'd have liked to have seen. Since its annexation to Great Britain, the feudal system of clans that had dominated the social structure had disappeared, and with it, the people of Scotland's lifestyle. They were forced to emigrate or flock to the large southern cities.

The writers made the journey together, but published their books separately: Johnson did so some two years later, in 1775; and Boswell published his in 1786, after Johnson's death. Without his subject realising it, the notes that Boswell made for *The Journal of a Tour to the Hebrides* also provided him with key material for *The Life of Samuel Johnson*. This is considered by many to be one of the best biographies ever written and is undoubtedly the book that revolutionised the genre from the moment it was published.

The Roca brothers have faithfully followed in the footsteps of Johnson and Boswell as far as culinary interest has allowed. The detours they made from the route and stop-offs of the eighteenth-century writers arc short digressions, which are justified because of the way in which these additional traditions, products and producers complete the tale.

A CULINARY BOOK WITH A DEBT TO TRAVEL JOURNALS

Johnson and Boswell's books cannot be considered to be culinary. They do mention food, products and customs in passing, just as any traveller does when coming into contact with an unfamiliar culture, out of curiosity for the new and to create a comparison with one's own reference points. For the eighteenth-century writers, the Highlands, West Coast and Hebrides seem as exotic and far away as countries thousands of miles away, despite their geographical proximity. Joan, Josep and Jordi focus on the culinary mentions in the books and, in creating their own journey, they explore these aspects to satisfy their curiosity. They're not the first to do so; Virginia Maclean did the same thing in 1973, with her book *Much Entertainment.*[2] Her book is, in fact, a collection of all the culinary references that appear in Johnson and Boswell's texts: these dishes that the travellers ate on their journey through the inns, houses and castles that received them and are described in their books. Maclean takes advantage of these references to include recipes and

2 Maclean, V. (1973), *Much Entertainment. A visual and Culinary Record of Johnson and Boswell's Tour of Scotland in 1773.* London: J.M. Dent & Sons Limited.

contextualises them with extracts from the eighteenth-century texts. In the places that the authors visited but didn't mention what they ate, Maclean chose recipes traditionally linked to these areas or to the products that were traditionally cultivated or foraged.

So this is a journey with a huge debt to various travel books. Again we see literature as the driving force behind adventures, as a spark for curiosity, making the reader want to experience for themselves what others have seen and written about. In fact, for Samuel Johnson and James Boswell, it was also through literature that they fell under the spell of this mystical land, in which the abrupt landscape, tricky terrain and severe climate seem to have surrounded the identity with a border that is impervious to time. Their reference books were Martin Martin's *A Description of the Western Islands of Scotland* (1703), in which the image portrayed matched the one that Johnson had had of Scotland since he was young; and the contemporary *A Tour in Scotland in 1769* by Thomas Pennant, which was published just a couple of years before the pair set out on their own journey. 'He's the best traveller I ever read; he observes more things than anyone else does,'[3] said Johnson of Pennant.

Scotland has a strong magnetic pull and, at the time, it fascinated travellers as much, if not more than it does today the thousands of tourists who visit every year. Perhaps it was this powerful effect that made the foreigners take out their notebooks while on the journey. Neither Samuel Johnson's book nor Virginia Maclean's, which were both sources of inspiration for the Roca brothers, had been planned beforehand. Maclean explains in her introduction that she decided to start writing while rereading Johnson's book during a trip around

3 Johnson, S. & Boswell, J. (2006). *A Journey to the Western Islands of Scotland and the Journal of a Tour to the Hebrides.* London: Penguin Classics.

THE ROCA BROTHERS APPROACH SCOTTISH CUISINE CAREFULLY AND TACTFULLY, IN THE HUMBLE AND RESPECTFUL WAY USED WHEN COMING INTO CONTACT WITH SOMETHING THAT IS APPRECIATED. THEY INTEND TO WITNESS, ARE EXCITED TO INTERPRET AND WANT TO LEARN FROM EVERYTHING THEY HAVE SEEN ON THEIR JOURNEYS. THE NEW KNOWLEDGE THEY ACQUIRE WILL BECOME AN INVALUABLE SOURCE OF INSPIRATION AS A RECIPE BOOK.

Scotland with her husband and three American friends. As for Johnson, his book describes the exact moment in which he came up with the idea of a book, 'I sat down on a bank [...] the day was calm, the air soft, and all was rudeness, silence and solitude. Before me, and on either side, were high hills [...] here I first conceived the thought of this narration.'[4] These reflections were made in Glen Shiel, a short while after leaving Fort Augustus, two weeks into the trip.

From the very start of the trip, Joan, Josep and Jordi share a notebook in which they jot down notes about the places they visit and the people they meet, keeping a record of the thoughts and feelings evoked by what they see and taste. But they still hadn't come up with the idea of writing a book: it was just a notebook in which they collected and shared information from the five journeys they made separately. Later on, these five trips, made on different occasions between March 2017 and February 2018, would structure the book into five chapters. The decision to write came about along the way, when they realised how interesting the material was that they were gathering. The discovery of new products, conversations with people who are passionate about the primary products and the countryside, and the contact with eager chefs inspired the brothers and made them realise what a good idea it would be to compile it in order.

---

4 Johnson, S. (1984). *A Journey to the Western Islands of Scotland*. London: Penguin Classics.

CROSSING PATHS; WEAVING TOGETHER THREADS

The book starts by weaving together different threads: the main part of the story is the trip, the anti-clockwise route that starts in Edinburgh and follows Johnson and Boswell's almost-three-month journey. This journey is depicted in the book through the writers' descriptions, analyses and thoughts about the Scotland of that time. In some cases they are just anecdotes; in others, they give important information to provide a better understanding of the Scotland through which the Roca brothers are travelling. The trips undertaken by Joan, Josep and Jordi are the other thread of this story, the part that covers the culinary aspect of the route, through contact with the landscape and its people. For this part, most of the information is provided by testimonials they collected and the brothers' *in situ* or *a posteriori* reflections. Joan is the protagonist of the first trip, which takes place in Edinburgh and the surrounding area with a venture into the Scottish Borders. Josep then takes over, carrying out three of the trips and travelling through practically the whole country: first, the east coast, then the north and the Shetland Islands, and lastly the Isle of Mull and part of the west coast. In between, Jordi visits Skye and Raasay, two of the Inner Hebrides; and travels to the centre of the country — on a detour — to visit a couple of producers. The Shetland Islands, far off the north coast at 60 latitude north, weren't on Johnson and Boswell's route either, but the Up Helly Aa[5] celebration makes Josep change his plan.

5 A fire festival celebrated on the Shetland Islands every year on the last Tuesday of January. They started in the nineteenth century and refer to the Viking culture that is present on the islands.

Joan, Josep and Jordi in front of The Macallan New Distillery

The last thread that makes up the book are forty recipes. They are distributed throughout the chapters based on different criteria: in some cases, these are recipes from one of the places that has been covered in the chapter. In others, they originate in the link between a product or producer and the geographical area covered on this specific trip. Sometimes they are recreations of recipes that Johnson and Boswell mentioned in their books and that Virginia Maclean collected in hers. The resulting recipe book is the fruit of two pieces of work: first, an immersion — the trips — to get to know the country's cuisine; then, the creative development process, carried out at La Masia.[6] In this second part the Roca brothers pay a tribute to Scottish cuisine, using stimuli like tradition, landscape, research, the product, innovation, poetry, daring or sense of humour.

6 La Masia is a space just a few metres from El Celler in which interdisciplinary research, creativity and training are carried out in association with the restaurant.

A BOOK THAT COMES INTO BEING ALONG THE WAY

'If only [the stone] could speak, it could tell me its history in the blink of an eye; if it could just open up I could get to the heart of this country immediately... It would be like distilling Scotland into a beaker!' fantasises Joan Roca, recently arrived in Edinburgh. The recently arrived traveller's desire to know everything about a new place as soon as they arrive is a fantasy and, at the same time, a test of their will to understand the keys to the reality awaiting them. Over time, the Roca brothers achieved this aim, after a year of visits and the additional time it took to prepare the trips and complete the work that followed it, processing the collected information. The result, essentially, is this book. It is impossible to distil a country and its cuisine using the laws of physics. If this method worked, the trip and everything that led up to it, the protagonists, the context in which they act and their opinions would have been devoid of meaning. Our real aim by distilling Scotland was to get an essence, but one obtained through passion, 'All stories first pass through the storyteller's filter and then that of the listener,' reflects Josep Roca. It is this subjectivity that makes the tale so interesting.

The project took shape as the Roca brothers discovered more about Scotland on successive trips. It is like the poet Antonio Machado's idea of the road being made by walking, which surely applies to any trip; but is especially fitting for this one: of course there was the initial idea, an intuition, a few expectations of the cuisine of a country that was traditionally a coastal larder for others. The Roca brothers have had professional links with Scotland for at least fifteen years, particularly Josep, because of the whisky; but he himself recognises that, until now, his culinary experience had only been 'that of a filling and

Vinegar barrels at the Edinburgh Food Studio

Fishing on the River Dee

comforting cuisine, associated with the cold climate'. And this is true, but today this is only part of what makes up Scottish cuisine. The wealth that they have witnessed on their trips confirms this fact: there are main ingredients that still underpin the food eaten in Scotland, such as cereals – oats are still used in many recipes, potatoes, tubers and dairy, used to make delicious butters and exceptional cheeses that still don't receive the recognition they deserve. 'It's a challenge working with austere products and the Scots are experts in turning this austerity into quality,' Jordi Roca observes while looking back on the trip. He's probably remembering the strawberries he became obsessed with and which encouraged him to take a detour from the planned route.

In Scotland, people have turned back to face the sea, to value products like the shellfish found along its coasts: succulent lobster, scallops, langoustines, oysters and mussels; and species of fish that have always been appreciated like salmon, cod, monkfish and haddock. There has been a change in attitudes, greater interest in what the land can provide, whether it be cultivated or foraged. The range of dishes that use lamb is endless, they use it as much as the Spanish use pig products. Recipes like haggis, a stuffed meat made with lamb's innards, which is a trademark dish of Scottish cuisine, reveal one of its other key characteristics: the approach of making the most of everything. The beef from native breeds tastes exquisite, and the wild game meat is so varied and of such a high quality that it makes Josep flirt with the idea — jokingly — of moving El Celler to Scotland for the hunting season.

In this attractive list of ingredients everything is Scottish and everything falls within the generic idea of what is to be found in the Scottish larder. Furthermore, many of them can be found in other surrounding cuisines. It's true that potatoes came from South America, but they have been rooted in Europe for centuries. We could say the same about the spices, from Asia, that are used to season haggis. So what then is new, if anything? There's no doubt that it's the interest in once again using local products. We say once again because, after decades of being undervalued, they had been forgotten. There are other products that are mentioned in the book that may seem more original, such as seaweed. But this is a false perception: the use of seaweed within cultures where it is abundant is age-old. In Scotland it was used as a fertiliser, as a raw material in the glass industry, and as feed for livestock. Also, it's been used for human consumption: there is evidence of it at least since the times that Neolithic people lived in the Orkney Islands, and recipes for dulse seaweed soup can often be found in traditional recipe books. It stopped being consumed when the land stopped being cultivated, at the same moment that knowledge started to be lost about the use of wild herbs: when the rural areas emptied. Foraging plants, flowers and shoots was a usual task in the eighteenth century. Perhaps the novelty today lies in the fact that this foraging is now carried out for the most sophisticated restaurants.

PEOPLE HAVE TO BELIEVE IN IT

Just as Johnson and Boswell crossed Scotland in the late eighteenth century, during a time of great change, Joan, Josep and Jordi are certain that they are documenting a turning point in Scottish cuisine. The eighteenth-century writers witnessed the last days of a country whose face of society had started to change with the arrival of the Industrial Revolution. The brothers, through speaking to chefs, producers and foragers, see that an appreciation of the culinary potential of their own country is starting to grow that, until recently, was practically inexistent. It is surprising to see, for example, that in some areas chefs still find it hard to come by the excellent fish and shellfish caught by their fishermen. All of them, without exception, say that for decades the best Scottish raw materials have found their way to places where they were appreciated more, and therefore, were more lucrative: principally France, Spain and Italy. For this emerging change to take place, the established patterns have to be broken. This task is within reach of a generation that has started to get the ball rolling, with some precedents over the last decade. The testimony of some of these figures is also compiled in the book. The first results can already be seen; the future looks promising.

'Everything is set for Scottish cuisine to see an exponential development,' forecast the Roca brothers. The high quality of the ingredients, the passion of those who grow, forage or process them, the qualities of the Scottish landscape, the healthy economy, the fascinating mixture of cultures it has inherited and with which, in recent years, it continues to be enriched, its attraction as a tourist destination... All the elements are there. What else is needed? 'They just need to believe in it!' Joan, Josep and Jordi reply in unison. There have been culinary revolutions built on weaker foundations, 'Why hasn't it happened here yet?' they ask themselves. From the deck of the ferry to the Isle of Mull, on the last trip, Josep Roca writes and, perhaps without intending to do so, answers the question, 'The light in the north filters diagonally through the clouds. It's as if it were asking for permission, shy and fleeting. It is quick to withdraw, turning towards introspection. It is somehow comforting and character-building. The culture and cuisine of this country are also shaped by these beams of light that cut through the slanted atmosphere.'

The Roca brothers approach Scottish cuisine carefully and tactfully, in the humble and respectful way used when coming into contact with something that is appreciated. They intend to witness, are excited to interpret and want to learn from everything they have seen on their journeys. The new knowledge they acquire will become an invaluable source of inspiration as a recipe book. Product tastings, dishes in restaurants or in the unlikeliest of settings, and conversations with the specialists and enthusiasts they meet along the way have made their mark. On their return to El Celler, after the necessary rest, the ideas for dishes paying tribute to Scotland start to flow in abundance. What stems from this emotion is inspiring: the forty recipes in this book are a tribute to the excellent products the brothers encountered, an innocent interpretation of dishes that probably only a few foreigners have tasted, they sing a tale of tradition and a search for union between these two culinary cultures that are so different: the Mediterranean and Atlantic at parallel 60.

This book wouldn't exist without the useful travel journals that came before it. James Boswell, who had the idea of writing his journal from the very start, noted the ups and downs and anecdotes of their journey in his diary. Doctor Johnson asked him to read it to him from time to time. On other occasions, he read the diary without asking or peered over Boswell's shoulder as he was writing. At one point, while they were in the Hebrides, the doctor expressed his admiration, because he liked what Boswell was writing more and more. In the same way, Joan, Josep and Jordi look through each brother's notes in the notebook they shared during the trip. Like Johnson, each time they enjoy what they're reading a little more. It's a distillation of Scotland.

Sheep grazing near Kilninver

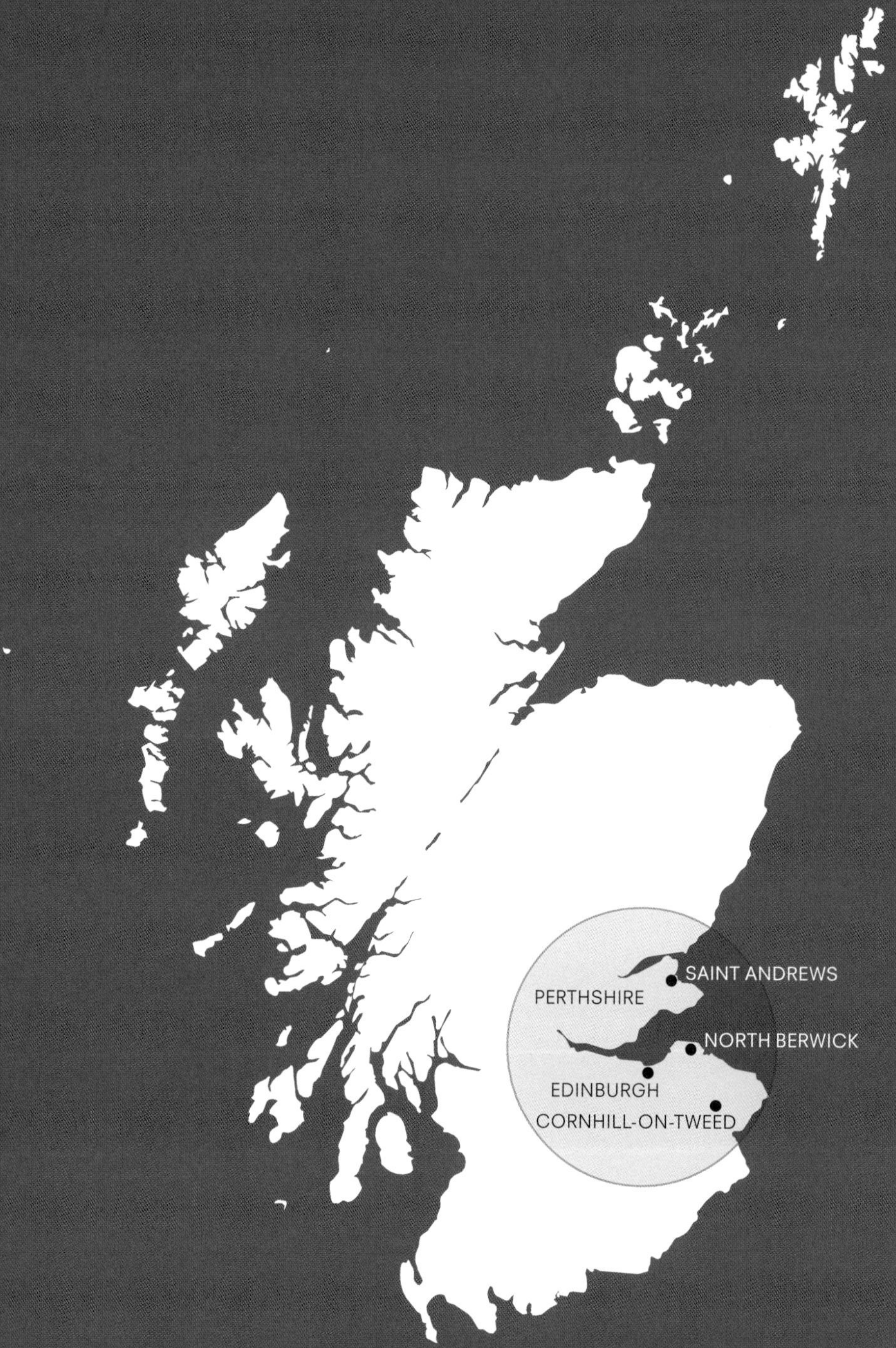

SAINT ANDREWS
PERTHSHIRE
NORTH BERWICK
EDINBURGH
CORNHILL-ON-TWEED

EDINBURGH, THE SURROUNDING AREA AND THE SCOTTISH BORDERS

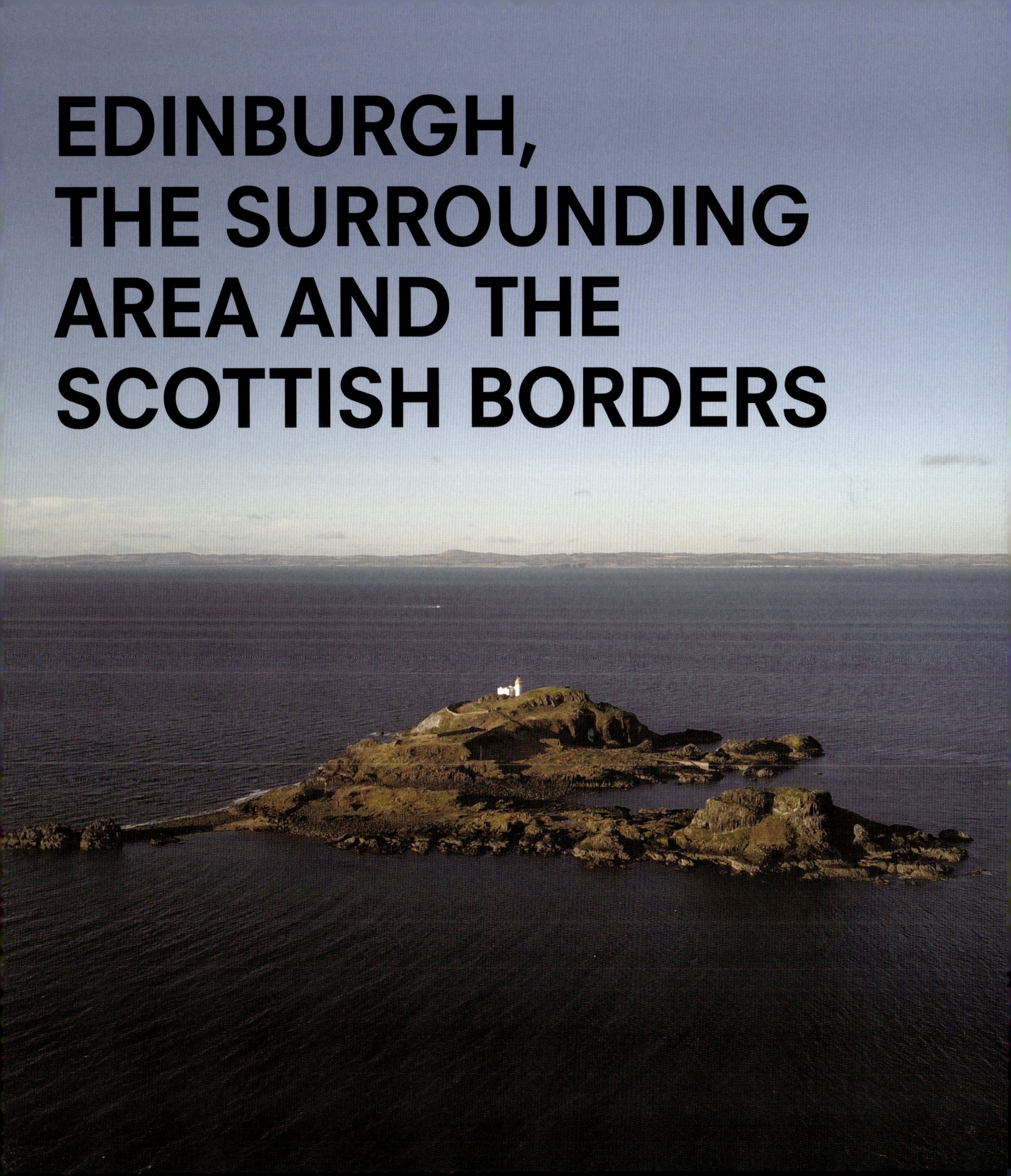

The Forth Bridge near Edinburgh
Previous page: Fidra, an island in the Firth of Forth, from the air

For ten years, the writer James Boswell had been waiting for his friend, fellow writer Samuel Johnson, to arrive in Edinburgh, to finally start out on a promising and long-awaited tour through Scotland. On the night of his arrival, 14 August 1773, Boswell went to collect him at Boyd's Inn, a ten-minute walk from his house in James Court, where he was living with his wife. The return trip was made arm-in-arm down the High Street on the main road of the Old Town; at the time, this was the only part of Edinburgh that had yet been built.

During the writers 83-day trip through Scotland, on the outskirts of Edinburgh, at Craigleith quarry, hundreds of men were working hard to build the New Town. This image is symbolic of what was happening in the country: alongside this enlightened urban expansion plan with its Georgian houses, rural Scotland was crumbling, and a new economic and social fabric was being woven. Scotland was an early adopter, and mere decades after the Union with England, the country was irreversibly entering into the Industrial Revolution. With the first groups of emigrants setting sail for the Americas, the countryside was emptying and the cities growing in population and size. Johnson and Boswell, careful witnesses to the changing times, set out on their trip to document a Scotland that was in the process of disappearing.

Joan, Edinburgh

Amongst the stream of tourists walking down the Royal Mile — as the old High Street is named today — I'm looking for these two friends: the proud host finally receiving the long-awaited visit of his eminent English colleague and the recently arrived guest, curious and dazzled, full of doubts and questions, with some clear ideas and a few prejudices in mind. I look to connect to this feeling felt by any outsider arriving in a new place, however warm the welcome and dear the friend who offers it. Also, I'm sure that Scotland has been waiting for a long time, perhaps even more than ten years!

I look upon the face of the city as a complete foreigner. For the moment, I'm unable to penetrate further than the outer layer: Edinburgh is built from dark grey sandstone. It is an elegant city, the buildings' height is restrained and the various hills upon which it is built provide a bird's eye view, as if it were a mass of small urban nuclei packed with monuments: towers, domes, spires and slate-coloured rooftops.

Having passed St Giles' Cathedral, I escape the crowds down one of the alleyways that opens up beneath the houses, between souvenir shops. I walk for a few metres under the beams of the building and come out into a small inner square flanked by ancient, peaceful and scarcely-visited houses: this is James Court, but I can't find any evidence to indicate which was James Boswell's house. I walk around the perimeter of the square a couple of times and end up leaning on one of the walls. This stone that I'm touching! If only it could speak, it could tell me its history in the blink of an eye; if it could just open up I could get to the heart of this country immediately... It would be like distilling Scotland into a beaker!

Joan at the Edinburgh Food Studio

‘IF YOU LOOK AT THE WEATHER, IT AFFECTS EVERYTHING, THE CLIMATE TELLS YOU WHAT TO COOK.’

—PAUL KITCHING

'SCOTLAND COOKS WINTER BEST'

Ben Reade is Joan Roca's Edinburgh guide. For a little over two years, with Sashana Souza, he has been running the Edinburgh Food Studio, a crowd-funded project that doubles as a restaurant and research hub. He seems to have an insatiable curiosity about anything to do with cuisine and his perspective of it is both broad and grounded. The doors to his studio are wide open to generate and share knowledge: as well as the normal dynamic of a restaurant, he often invites chefs from around the world who are sending a message through their cuisine. Ben spent a long time working in Copenhagen as the Head of Culinary Research at the Nordic Food Lab before deciding to return to his home country. Amongst his recent projects, one stands out: he has travelled around the country documenting Scottish culinary customs and curiosities, gathering oral histories. In fact, he has already made contact with these day-to-day voices that will help Joan to get a grasp on Scottish cuisine, from his Mediterranean perspective.

> *'If you look at the weather, it affects everything, the climate tells you what to cook'. This is how Paul Kitching, chef at the restaurant 21212, answered the question that, up until now, seems unfathomable to me: 'How can Scottish cuisine be defined?'. Paul's answer is in line with the idea that a cuisine is a territory and the inescapable link that this has with its climate. 'Scotland cooks winter best,' he says. If, as my fellow countryman Josep Pla wrote, the cuisine of a country 'is its landscape put into a casserole', cooking its climate means remaining true to what the landscape offers at any given moment. In other words: local and seasonal products, the unfailing sacrosanct of our profession. Cuisine has*

always been a trustworthy way of sketching the outline of a community. It's true that it's not the most scientific method, but it certainly defines collective identities. We are shaped by the language we speak – and how we speak it, by what we eat and drink – and how we eat and drink it, and by little more.

On the dawn of the Industrial Revolution, when Johnson and Boswell were setting out on their journey, the landscape, what it produced, who was cultivating it and what those who lived in it ate formed the harmoniously overlapping layers of a shared identity. Or perhaps this is just a romantic idea. 'Haggis, the standard bearer of Scotland's culinary identity is probably adapted from a Roman recipe while its name comes from Old Norse (*hǫggva* meaning to hack/chop). Besides the offal, animal fat, oats and vegetables that go into haggis, all of which can be found in Scotland itself, another key ingredient is the spices which are grown on the other side of the world! Nor are the traditional accompaniments to haggis any more Scottish than black pepper: neeps (swedes) are most likely of Swedish origin while tatties (potatoes) of course came from the New World.'[1] Ben Reade wrote this in one of the articles on his blog and it pours cold water over the poetic way in which the dish is described when the aim is to convert it into the folkloric symbol of a national identity.

1 Haggis Tikka Masala. Edinburgh Food Studio, 29 March 2017. Accessed 29 December 2017. Available at http://www.edinburghfoodstudio.com/blog/2016/12/29/haggis-tikka-masala.

Ben Reade, chef of the Edinburgh Food Studio, and Gary Goldie, forager

Of course, memory is short. When, at El Celler we use it as inspiration, it rarely goes back further than what our grandparents ate, but for us this already represents a whole lifetime; we usually end up reinventing the dishes of our childhood. When we believe that memory is shared and common, that identifying with a recipe goes beyond a family level, then we talk about tradition, our tradition. These references that we believe are shared are another of the sparks that ignite our creativity. Both are sources of inspiration and truly connect us to an identity. But what kind of identity? Here I turn to the historian and gastronome Massimo Montanari when he says that identities aren't written in stone, 'The quest for roots, when undertaken with a critical methodology, and not screened behind impulsive emotional associations, never succeeds in defining our point of departure. On the contrary, we find instead a web of increasingly denser threads, ever broader and more complicated that recede from us. Within this intricate system of relationships and exchanges, it is not the roots but ourselves who are the fixed point: identity does not exist at the outset but rather at the end of the trajectory.'[2]

---

2 Montanari, M. (2006). *Food is Culture*. New York City: Columbia University Press.

‘SCOTTISH PRODUCTS ARE NOW THE PROTAGONISTS OF THE MENU.’

—JOAN ROCA

Joan Roca with Sandy Patullo of Eassie Farm

USE THE PRODUCTS YOU HAVE AROUND YOU

With the experience he has behind him and the generation that he belongs to, Andrew Radford is a veteran of what could be considered as the foundations of modern Scottish cuisine. ‘How have you seen Edinburgh evolve in terms of cuisine?’ asks Ben, who, given his age, could be one of Andrew’s sons. The question doesn’t surprise Andrew, seemingly it’s not the first time that he’s been asked. ‘Twenty-five years ago, if a chef went to the Scottish coast to buy langoustines, they wouldn’t find them anywhere: they were all exported to France and Spain,’ he recalls. In other words, Scottish chefs couldn’t easily access the incredible raw materials produced right on their doorstep. Whether it was because they were undervalued, or because others valued them more and the — harsh — law of the market sent them to places that were more profitable, the custom of eating certain products just didn’t exist and, therefore, an internal market hadn’t developed around them.

Around a table at Timberyard, the family restaurant where his sons manage the kitchen and dining room, Andrew tells an idyllic story about producers of a certain period, some 34 years ago. This was a time in which nobody mentioned sustainability, Km0 products, or expressions like ‘from field to fork’ in agriculture and trade, let alone in catering. ‘The first time I worked in kitchens was aboard The Royal Scotsman, a luxury train that travelled almost the entire Scottish rail network. The train toured the country every two weeks. Suppliers knew the train’s timetable and would come up to the train to sell their products, I’m talking about the early 1980s here!’. Today, all non-alcoholic drinks served in the restaurant are made on site, with local aromatic herbs, flowers and fruit.

It takes me a while to understand the logic of Andrew's answer and to make the connection between what he has just said and Ben's question. However, it is a powerful example. My first meals in Edinburgh restaurants confirm that a change in this direction is taking place: Scottish products are now the protagonists of the menu. Therefore, the example that Andrew gave to explain the city's culinary evolution is very telling of what has happened in a short time.

Tom Kitchin, another of the most renowned chefs in the city, welcomes his diners to their table with a map of Scotland featuring all of the products found on his menu. Furthermore, the way in which a dish is described on the menu, the order of elements, the hierarchy between the ingredients, what is highlighted and what doesn't even appear are all details that say a lot about the philosophy behind each restaurant. The menu at Tom's restaurant The Kitchin is crystal clear in this regard: there's one line with the main ingredient — no embellishment — and a short explanation on a second line about where the recipe's main and secondary ingredients come from. This is a clear sign that the times have changed. One of his dishes combines oysters, langoustines, mussels, prawns and cockles in the same dish. It's a small tribute to the products that can be harvested around the Scottish coast at low tide. Today, at long last, these are valued as they should be on the local market.

As I stroll through Edinburgh, it strikes me that there are hardly any fishmongers in the city. I find one, in the neighbourhood of Stockbridge, where they tell me about another specialised in shellfish on the other side of the city, and a third in Leith Harbour. It's not many for a city of half a million inhabitants. Not when you take into account the numbers in Spain, where a deep-rooted culture of eating fish is keeping the small trade of the fishmongers alive. It's not the first time that this question has crossed my mind, the suspicion that countries gifted with miles and miles of coastline don't make the most of the natural larder this provides them with. Don't the Scottish eat fish? Do they only eat it in restaurants? Or perhaps they do eat it at home, but buy it in supermarkets? I'll keep this question in mind to see if I can find some more clues during my trip.

Perhaps today's restaurants have become strongholds where the home-cooked dishes of the past are showcased and brought up to date. Ben illustrates this hypothesis with the example of game, 'The percentage of families that say they cook with game is ridiculously low and nobody cooks venison at home. However, much of traditional Scottish cuisine is often linked to game.' He makes his view on the topic clear, 'Sometimes I buy a pheasant for the restaurant for one pound. Making the most of it, it provides two people with four meals. What poor families normally eat is far more expensive.' The problem, therefore, is unfamiliarity and there is a strong need to create an educative plan to reverse the situation.

I accompany Ben to George Bower Butchers, a small local shop that specialises in game and cold meats. I was really pleased to see the counter; at first glance, you could tell that the produce was of high quality. It's the type of place where you get the feeling of belonging to a culinary identity, in this case, one that is different to my own. 'They're the customers and restaurants in the neighbourhood's favourite sausages', the owner explains, gesturing to some of the selection on offer. 'These are lamb and mint, those ones are venison and garlic and the others are wild boar with apple and parsley.' For the first time since setting foot in the country, a variety of haggis hang before me, some stuffed into what must be a sheep's stomach, others in strings, like botifarra (Catalan sausage), stuffed into intestines. 'They are made with lung, heart, liver and kidney; also, we add some skirt steak to increase the meat content and add some fat. A couple of times a week a retired sausage maker, with plenty of experience, comes to make the cured meats in the traditional way.'

Faced with my curiosity, the owner very kindly takes us to the basement where the smoke house and the skinning and meat maturing areas are found. 'I have to prepare a roe deer for Tom Kitchin. He likes to buy whole pieces of meat to use them exactly as he likes and get the most possible meat out of them,' he says, implicitly inviting us to watch the skinning process. Ben warns me not to blink an eye. Indeed, with ten expert movements, the piece, that was hung from a door beam, becomes skinned, lying on the sacrificial altar. A string of rabbits and hares of different sizes witness the mastery of the knife, awaiting their turn. Before leaving Bower's we choose a few birds to take with us for a tasting at Edinburgh Food Studio, to which Ben has also invited Gary Goldie.

YOU CAN FORAGE ANYWHERE

Goldie arrives at Ben's kitchen laden with seaweeds and herbs. He's an interesting guy, one of these people who has taken the opposite route to that of the product: he has moved from the kitchen to the field and is now a supplier of wild products for restaurants. He could be called a gatherer. It may sound like something from ancient times, but he has made a livelihood out of this traditional way of living. The role of gatherer has lost importance as a main supply source for restaurants, but it's never been completely lost. It seems like something that people are interested in reviving, seeing as it's also a way of regaining knowledge about the environment which, having turned our backs on nature, we'd forgotten. At El Celler de Can Roca, the biologist Evarist March is in charge of supplying the kitchen with wild plants and sharing his knowledge with the chefs. Joan calculates that since the start of this collaboration, through the project *Terra Animada* (Living Land), around a hundred species of plants have been added to the restaurant's dishes.

Gary explains and gives tasters of everything he has collected to chefs. He opens up plastic containers with different kinds of seaweed — all with different shapes and flavourings: pepper, oyster, mushrooms, etc. — while explaining how he harvested them, at low tide. Among the wide variety of plants he has collected, there is alexanders[3] with its aromatic flavours of orange and cardamom, whose seeds, once dried, can be used to make a citrus and balsamic dust for seasoning foods. His regular contact with kitchens and his experience — he explains that the idea for what he does now came

3 *Smyrnium olusatrum*.

from doing an internship at the Noma restaurant (Copenhagen) — means that he also processes some of the foods that he forages. It's what he does, for example, with the garlic and wild leek seed pods that form once the flower has fallen. After salting and pickling them in vinegar he obtains something similar to capers, but with a different taste.

In Newington cemetery I come to the realisation that you can literally forage anywhere. At Gary's suggestion and with Ben's involvement, we enter the graveyard just a few metres down the road from the restaurant. It's not so much the idea of foraging in a cemetery that bothers me, but that of taking from the world of the dead to benefit the living. However, my reservations, probably cultural in nature, quickly disappear on entering because Newington is closer to this world than our cemeteries are. Although the mausoleums remind me that I'm walking on sacred ground, the size of the place, the pathways, easy access from the urban routine and naturalness with which people stroll through the cemetery make me feel like I'm in a park somewhere on the threshold between both worlds. The crosses of some tombs have fallen with time, there are Romantic sculptures lying face down in the grass and some of the tombstones have cracked naturally due to the weather. It's true that the atmosphere is inevitably gloomy, but birdsong filters through the funerary architecture as Ben hands Gary some bearberries.[4]

---

4 *Arctostaphylos uva-ursi.*

ON THE DAWN OF THE
INDUSTRIAL REVOLUTION,
WHEN JOHNSON AND
BOSWELL WERE SETTING
OUT ON THEIR JOURNEY,
THE LANDSCAPE, WHAT
IT PRODUCED, WHO WAS
CULTIVATING IT AND WHAT
THOSE WHO LIVED IN IT ATE
FORMED THE HARMONIOUSLY
OVERLAPPING LAYERS OF
A SHARED IDENTITY.
OR PERHAPS THIS IS JUST
A ROMANTIC IDEA.

Razor clams. Smoked haddock. Game birds. Varieties of potatoes grown in Scotland

On returning from the cemetery, Ben starts preparing the birds for the tasting session. The aim of the session is to identify nuances and textures, so he has decided to avoid unnecessary frills. However, he hasn't been able to avoid the temptation of making some tattie scones, which may be the Scottish substitute toasted bread; there are also some oatcakes on hand. In a frying pan, he carefully browns each piece of deboned poultry in butter, cooking it to its optimum point. Next, he sets them aside on a tray until they are all ready. There are three types of duck, wild partridge and wood pigeon. 'You can start with any you like, it's entirely up to you,' Ben challenges.

The partridge has a very interesting taste, you can tell that it has grown eating wild foods. It's incomparable to the bred partridges that we normally eat, although it's true, as Ben says, that it is a white meat, with the same range of flavours that can be found in a chicken or quail. After, we try a teal,[5] the smallest of the three ducks on offer, it seems that it's the hardest one to get hold of and, therefore, the most highly valued. It has a delicate nutty taste and metallic nuances. The following ducks, the mallard[6] and widgeon,[7] don't interest me so much, they're more common, with perhaps more familiar tastes. However, the wood pigeon captivates me! Ben has cooked it very lightly, which is probably the best way to eat it. It's delicious! I ask about the traditional way to cook it, if there is one. 'Pigeon pie!' he exclaims. Then, before explaining any further, he takes a Scottish recipe book off the shelf and shows me an endless list of recipes with pigeon as their main ingredient.

---

5 *Anas discors.*

6 *Anas platyrhynchos.*

7 *Anas penelope.*

Seeing Joan's interest, Ben explains that throughout the United Kingdom, and especially in Scotland, there have been pigeon lofts since the Middle Ages. Some houses in the city had a hole in the roof for pigeons to enter. However, permission to have a pigeon loft, generally given to the wealthy, was only awarded by the king. Anyone who was given this privilege very soon realised that owning pigeons was an easy way to steal the working classes' grain, as the birds always returned home with their throats full. To make sure that the working classes didn't take revenge, or simply kill the birds for their meat, 'there were periods of Scottish history in which shooting birds was punishable by death,' explains Ben.

OATS AND POTATOES: TWO PILLARS OF SUBSISTENCE COOKING

Although the main aim was to try the birds, Joan can't ignore the tattie scones and oatcakes that he's been nibbling at between one piece of meat and the next. Potato and oats, these are two of the symbolic ingredients of Scottish culture. One, a cereal, has been present as a staple food since the Middle Ages; the other, a tuber, is a recent arrival that didn't start setting down roots until the mid-eighteenth century. Samuel Johnson describes oats in his dictionary as 'a grain, which in England is generally given to horses, but in Scotland supports the people.'[8] The breakfasts and meals mentioned in his travel journal confirm this. There aren't many houses or inns in which oats aren't served in one of their traditional forms: oatcakes, porridge, in stuffing or as a crust for a fish pie. When they are on the Isle of Skye, just about to leave Talisker, they enter a house where a woman is grinding oats between two stones. This cereal seems to be the only one, along with, to a lesser extent, rye, that can withstand the humidity and low sunlight conditions of the Highlands and Western Isles.

There aren't so many mentions of potatoes in the writers' books. Despite its rapid expansion once it became established as a crop in Scotland, in 1773, hardly two generations had grown potatoes. Its persistence and ability to grow in the poorest conditions turned it, thanks to its high nutritional value, into the staple food for more deserted areas. Scotland probably owes as much to the potato that arrived from the Americas as Ireland does. However, both countries suffered to almost the same extent when, from 1846, potato blight devastated the crops. The dispossessed of the earth, who had put all their

8 Johnson, S. (1755). *A Dictionary of the English Language*. London: J. & P. Knapton.

‘IF ONLY [THE STONE] COULD SPEAK, IT COULD TELL ME ITS HISTORY IN THE BLINK OF AN EYE; IF IT COULD JUST OPEN UP I COULD GET TO THE HEART OF THIS COUNTRY IMMEDIATELY… IT WOULD BE LIKE DISTILLING SCOTLAND INTO A BEAKER!’

—JOAN ROCA

Anthony Carroll of Carroll's Heritage Potatoes

Lucy Carroll of Carroll's Heritage Potatoes

faith in the potato crop as a staple food, paid with hunger, disease and death. The countryside became deserted once again: some emigrated to Nova Scotia, while others found refuge in the Lowlands.

I've read that three fifths of Scottish land is unsuitable for growing crops. The mountains and lakes that are so iconic of Scotland's landscape and make it so beautiful render the land impractical for agriculture. One exception is the river valleys that extend towards Hadrian's Wall. This monument, in England, is the physical border and symbolic submission point where the Romans marked the limits of their empire. Unfaithful to Johnson and Boswell's journey, which never went further south than the imaginary line between Glasgow and Edinburgh, I accompany Michael Innes (Mike to us), a Scottish chef and friend who worked with us at El Celler, towards the banks of the River Tweed, the border with England. At Tiptoe Farm, near Cornhill-on-Tweed, we visit Lucy and Anthony, owners of Carroll's Heritage Potatoes. The reason that justifies this detour from the route is what they've been doing here over the last 20 years: planting potatoes. Not any old potatoes, as they had previously grown, but rather, tuber varieties especially chosen for their taste.

'Everything started when a distributor asked my husband to grow a specific variety of potato. Anthony wanted to know what the purpose was, what this potato tasted like and why they wanted him to grow it,' explains Lucy. However, the distributor replied that the taste wasn't that important. This event, which took place in 2000, was an alarm bell for the couple, who thought, in actual fact, that what the distributor had dismissed, the taste, was in fact the only thing that gave growing potatoes any meaning. They

started carrying out tests with different varieties, taken from the market gardeners of the area. At first, they grew only small amounts of Arran Victory, Pink Fir Apple, Red Duke of York and Red King Edward. 'When we started selling them at local markets we noticed that people loved the taste and on the following week they returned for more,' recalls Lucy. Today, they produce 17 varieties, some recovered from the Scottish government's seed bank, without which they would probably have already disappeared. 'They're not easy to grow, that's why nobody does so: they're irregular, with different sizes and eyes. The food industry doesn't like them,' says Anthony. However, it's the wealth of tastes, colours, shapes, textures and history behind each of them that makes them unique.

The business as it currently operates started around the farmhouse kitchen table with potato tastings followed by calls to chefs to see whether they might be interested in their product. 'It is constant work, over the years we've developed more understanding about the use of each variety and I'm continuously cooking them, so I can explain to the chefs what I like to do with each type. My favourite variety is Mr Little's Yetholm Gypsy!' confesses Lucy. This is a striking potato with red, white and purplish skin and ivory flesh. Right there, in the kitchen, Mike and Joan taste some of the varieties the couple have prepared. On Anthony's recommendation, they are boiled as he believes this is the best way to eat them. The two most striking varieties are Mayan Gold, the first potato to arrive from Peru, with its golden flesh, floury texture and addictive flavour; and Arran Victory, a variety from the west coast of Scotland, with purple skin and white flesh, used to make one of the lightest, airiest potato purées.

PLANTING LOBSTERS IN THE SEA

We return towards the north through a carpet of yellow fields. These are rape crops, a plant that is used to produce rapeseed oil: a common vegetable oil at these latitudes. We follow the east coast to arrive at North Berwick where the mouth of the River Forth flows into the North Sea. Upriver there is Edinburgh and on the other side of the estuary, just opposite, Kinghorn. In the middle is Inchkeith, a small island presided over by a lighthouse. When the writers stopped on the island, the day they took the ferry crossing north, Johnson said, 'Inchkeith is nothing more than a rock covered with a thin layer of earth, not wholly bare of grass, and very fertile of thistles.'[9] I'm eager to follow their footsteps, but a few important things hold me back on this shore.

Scotland is a major producer and exporter of shellfish. The majority of lobster catches are made in the Hebridean and Orkney islands and in the south-east, the area the chefs are currently visiting. Jane McMinn, director of the Firth of Forth Lobster Hatchery, welcomes Joan and Mike and explains the hard work that they have been carrying out since 2010. In this year they opened a small container in which they informed the few people who came at first to listen of the importance of encouraging sustainable coastal fisheries. For the people behind the hatchery, this is the most effective way to ensure the future of fishing and the livelihoods of those who depend on it. With the persistence

9 Johnson, S. (1984). *A Journey to the Western Islands of Scotland*. London: Penguin Classics.

of those who believed in the cause and a little funding, what in the beginning had been an awareness campaign for fishermen, schoolchildren and local people, became a reality: a lobster hatchery in which these crustaceans are protected during their most vulnerable stages. 'We work with local fishermen who bring us the female lobsters when they are laden with eggs. Each female lobster carries up to twenty thousand eggs. Out of these, in the open sea, only one would develop fully. Our initial calculations have shown that the hatchery's success rate is of 300,' Jane explains. The complete process lasts some three months. Once the eggs hatch, the lobster larvae pass through a system of tanks with constantly moving water. This process usually takes eight weeks, during which time the lobster sheds its skin three times. 'After the third moult, we transfer them to individual containers because, as a cannibal species, at this stage they would eat each other.' When they have grown enough they are transferred to acclimatisation tanks. The last step is the release onto the seabed, in which specialised divers dive with the juvenile lobsters and place them in protected areas of the bay.

WEEDS...

Before crossing the estuary of no return, I go back to the outskirts of Edinburgh. To continue the journey we have to cross the estuary over one of the bridges north of the city. In the no-man's-land of one of these transition zones between the countryside and the city, I meet Hamish Martin. He is a former wine merchant who, eight years ago, realised that his hobby until that moment, gardening, was about to become his life. He told me that one day, from the road, he saw the greenhouse in which I'm standing today. 'I leapt over the fence to enter the estate, there was no other way in. The greenhouse was in ruins but I liked the place. I left my telephone number with the neighbours who didn't even know who the owner was. Nine months later, I managed to enter and officially visit the place.' Hamish is another of these people who is extremely passionate about what he does. In what he calls the Secret Herb Garden, he grows 600 different types of herbs.

'We have beauty at our feet.' Hamish is quite obsessed with what everyone else would call weeds. His garden constitutes a return to the knowledge of the seventeenth century, when everyone knew a lot more about herbs and used them more than we do today. At the Secret Herb Garden salads are served with herbs, but also with weeds. 'How can nature be our enemy? The problem is that we just don't understand it! All the magic surrounding plants has been lost, we need to get closer to them, we're still so disconnected...' For this reason, some of the most welcome visitors are the schoolchildren from nearby Edinburgh. There's no specific business plan: they never planned to grow plants for restaurants, but now they supply 15 kitchens. Guest chefs come to cook at the Secret Herb Garden and they also host weddings, moonlit dinners and plant workshops.

I like what Hamish says about herbs and how he says it: this necessity of building a friendship with them. Dandelions are mentioned several times during the conversation, 'It's the most complete plant. It represents the entire universe: if you take its flower, trim it and hold it up against a blue sky, it's as if you are holding the sun between your fingers; if you hold a dandelion seed head up against the dark night sky you'll have a moon; blow and you'll see the stars!' While we stroll, he gives me some Sweet Cicely[10] *to try. We cross the flower gardens in which they grow 25 varieties of mint, tasting daisy petals, shepherd's purse, meadowsweet and clematis. Sorrel, marigold, wormwood, mugwort... Before saying goodbye, Hamish invites me to a delicate, aromatic mead that he made with cold plant infusions, his brother's honey and natural yeast. It's exquisite! My experience amongst the plants has been heady, the place transmits calmness and puts me into the best state of mind to leave Edinburgh behind and start out on my journey in the footsteps of Johnson and Boswell.*

---

10 *Myrrhis odorata.*

Hamish Martin of the Secret Herb Garden

Walking towards the car, I think that after a few days I still hadn't got to the core of Scotland. I'm still on the surface but with these first meetings and conversations with wonderful people I've already started to penetrate this first layer that foreigners encounter. I can now confirm what up until now had been a cliché: the Scottish are very hospitable. I've enjoyed writing notes so that, when Josep takes over, he will find my first impressions in this notebook, which without a doubt will ease his landing. 'Joan!' I hear Hamish's voice behind me. I turn around and see him coming towards me, a yellow flower in his hands, 'Look, it's wild cowslip. Do you recognise it? In Scotland it's a flower that is connected to the fairies. It's common to find it in the central reservations of the motorways. But if you see it in the woods, near mallows and other primroses, it means you're in a very special place. Take it with you on your journey!' I thank him for the little gift and we say goodbye again. On leaving the Secret Herb Garden I place the cowslip inside the cover of my notebook to keep it safe.

RAZOR CLAMS ON THE OTHER SIDE OF THE ESTUARY

Three enormous bridges cross the estuary between Edinburgh and Fife. None of these were built on 18 August 1773 when Johnson and Boswell left Leith Harbour by ferry to reach the other shore. A bird's eye view of the estuary reveals that the distance between the bridges is greater on the southern shore and they come together on the northern side. In this way, they form the image of a funnel that marks, as it narrows, the journey's destination. Although all three are impressive, it's hard to take your eyes off the Forth Bridge, the first to be built, in 1883. Even today, its steel engineering, recognised since 2015 as a UNESCO World Heritage Site, seems to challenge the laws of physics. Its cantilever, one of the longest ever to have been built, is still the route that railway traffic takes to cross from one side of the estuary to the other. It is the closest bridge to the river mouth. On the other side, there is the recently opened Queensferry Crossing, a modern and elegant bridge, built on three pillars, which spans the 2.7 kilometres separating the two shores and is the main route for vehicles, especially while the 1964 Forth Road Bridge, lying between the other two, is closed for maintenance.

When we arrive on the other side of the estuary night has almost fallen. Mike and Ben, who in the end have joined us from Edinburgh, accompany me. We travel a few kilometres along the coast, until we reach the beach where Rupert Waites is waiting for us to take us razor clam gathering. It's a wide sandy beach, the tide is out and the last rays of sunlight filter through the cobalt blue clouds that

'WHEN WE ARRIVE ON THE OTHER SIDE OF THE ESTUARY NIGHT HAS ALMOST FALLEN. MIKE AND BEN, WHO IN THE END HAVE JOINED US FROM EDINBURGH, ACCOMPANY ME.'
—JOAN ROCA

Ben Reade and Joan gathering razor clams on the Edinburgh coast

practically cover the sky. On the other shore, the lights of Edinburgh twinkle. It's one of those incredible moments in which, in the midst of absolute tranquillity, the only thing to be heard is the crackle of your own happiness.

Rupert is another chef-gatherer, although we could invert these words depending on whether they're put in chronological order — which came first — or whether they illustrate the weight of his two professions. Kitted out in wellington boots, a raincoat and carrying a wicker basket on his forearm, anyone could tell he was a shellfish catcher. Catching razor clams, which is what he's going to teach the three chefs, is complicated work. These bivalves are buried beneath the beach's sand and to get them to surface you have to bother them, sprinkling them with a saltwater solution. However, guessing where they are isn't an easy task. The most prized razor clams come from the coast and Western Islands, just like much of Scotland's molluscs and shellfish.

We fan out in a perpendicular line to the sea and walk backwards to comb the entire beach. The lack of light doesn't help with identifying where the razor clams might be buried. I look for shallow hollows in the sand with a slight bubbling and pour the salt water over. My first two attempts don't produce any results. But, third time lucky: I see something moving under the water I've just poured. Then, nothing. Then, suddenly, as if it were a submarine periscope, the shy tip of a razor clam appears. It's like an invitation to play, a 'you can't catch me!' from the little animal. And in fact, it's just about to slip away underground again when I pinch it with my fingers to pull it up completely.

It is pitch black. While the chefs finish filling the basket, Rupert has made a fire at one end of the beach. When the basket is full, they all sit around the fire and a lively conversation starts up. Over a trivet, Rupert heats an iron frying pan in which he melts a knob of butter and fries some alexanders.[11] Next, he opens the recently caught razor clams over the flash of direct flame required for them to open up. Off the heat, Rupert spreads some sea fennel shoots and pickled garlic cloves over the clams. The fire reflects the eager eyes of the chefs.

St Andrews is a university town. It remains so today and can boast about having the oldest university in Scotland, but when Johnson and Boswell visited this town, they didn't see it at its best. Johnson, a scholar who was concerned with education, described the state of the institution with dismay as, 'pining in decay and struggling for life'[12]. He complained bitterly that a prosperous nation, in which trade and wealth were increasing, had abandoned its commitment to educational institutions. Johnson's opinions about the university were not unfounded: for the two days they spent in St Andrews, the two travellers were hosted by one of the professors, so it's easy to imagine that the financial situation of the Academy might have come up in their conversations.

Despite the fact that on each of their stops Johnson and Boswell were received by a local person who knew the area well and guided them, they didn't always manage to visit what really interested them. Sometimes, as in St Andrews, this was out of lack of awareness. The time that passed between the journey and both writers' writing of their books allowed them to analyse the route and

---

11 *Smyrnium olusatrum.*

12 Johnson, S. (1984). *A Journey to the Western Islands of Scotland.* London: Penguin Classics.

realise that they hadn't visited the old St Rule's Church. Realising this loss, Boswell made a suggestion in his book that, made today, would be untimely, 'In every place, where there is any thing worthy of observation, there should be a short printed directory for strangers, such as we find in all the towns of Italy'.[13] The writer knew the country well because, a few years earlier, he had set out on another trip — taking him to France and Italy — about which he also wrote a book.[14]

13 Boswell, J. (1807). *The Journal of a Tour to the Hebrides*. London: T. Cadwell and W. Davies.

14 Boswell, J. *Boswell On the Grand Tour: Italy, Corsica and France, 1765-1766*.

CHEESES WITH A SCOTTISH FEEL

Ben Reade returns to Edinburgh and his Edinburgh Food Studio, whilst he leaves Joan and Mike on track for the St Andrews Farmhouse Cheese Company, a few kilometres away, where Jane Stewart is waiting for them. This artisan cheese-making company is still young, established in 2008, but is built on the foundations of a dairy farm in which three generations of the family have worked. Facing financial difficulties, with ever-decreasing profit margins in milk sales, they had to reinvent the business. Jane contacted a Welsh artisanal cheesemaker who had been making cheese successfully for 30 years and was about to retire. This man passed his know-how on to Jane and, with this in hand, she returned to Anstruther to launch the project.

Fife, where the farm is found, isn't a traditional cheese-producing region, so they had to start from scratch in every respect. Who knows if it is because of or in despite of this that they created their own niche in the local market. Their quick success there soon spread throughout the rest of the country. One of the key elements for guaranteeing the quality of the cheese is, without a doubt, the milk. The farm, which continues to operate at full capacity, guarantees complete control over this key raw material. The circle is complete because they also have land for growing cereals, meaning that part of the feed with which the cows are fed in winter, when they can't graze, is produced there. Jane explains that it's this connection with the environment that gives the cheeses their peculiar characteristics. The varieties they produce feature in the usual British typologies: the Anster, which was the first in a family that now includes another three cheeses, recalls the Cheshire cheeses that Jane's teacher

Joan at the Secret Herb Garden

taught her to make. It is smooth, lactic, with a faint, almost citric acidity and a brittle texture. Then there's the St Andrews Farmhouse Cheddar which is more rounded, creamy and strong. This is made using a cheddar-making method and is aged for one year.

At this point in the journey, after several days visiting cities, towns, farms and restaurants and after talking to producers, gatherers and chefs, I can see Scotland's culinary identity more clearly. I can see what has happened in the last few years and what is happening at the moment. Everyone that I've talked to is driven by their passion for what they're doing. In most cases they also have this vitality that comes with running young businesses. It seems as though a short time ago Scotland turned her gaze to look cuisine in its entirety in the face, just like this route that brings the product from the ground or the sea to the table. Having done so is an important and unmistakable gesture. It's these great passions, mostly played out in small businesses, that best reflect a change of mentality, a recently awakened interest, or perhaps, something that has been rediscovered in this wealth offered by this country.

Joan with Jane Stewart at the St Andrews Farmhouse Cheese Company

NEWCOMERS, BUT HERE TO STAY

Martine and Mohsin returned from Dubai to Perthshire and Mohsin's family home with one idea in mind: to produce the highest-quality meat. Since starting up Highland Wagyu, in 2011, they have devoted all their efforts towards this aim. One of their obsessions, convinced that it's the most determining factor in the meat quality, is the animals' genetics which creates the perfect cross between the wagyu breed and native Scottish breeds. They returned to the Scottish farm and created this project out of the love they both have for this Japanese breed and the meat it produces. It could be said that it was out of love for the fat as well, because it's the marbling of the fat that is a sign of excellence and what they always look for in their animals. It is also thanks to careful genetic selection that they have achieved, in their words, 'Angus cattle that are like the originals of this breed'. To do so, they have had to turn to North America, where the livestock arrived with the first immigrants and hasn't deteriorated to the same extent as in the UK. Used to working with fresh wagyu meat, one of the products that most strikes the chefs is the cold meat like salami, cured meats, bresaola and pastrami made from the lower quality cuts of meat. The taste, texture and fats are exceptional. 'The market always demands the same thing, but I prefer a lower quality cut of wagyu than the highest quality of other breeds,' explains Mohsin, referring to the usual mistake of not appreciating quality in itself, but rather the value of specific cuts.

Holstein cows at the St Andrews Farmhouse Cheese Company

On the last stretch of my journey, to visit a green asparagus producer near Glamis, I remember what Ben Reade told me about vegetable consumption in Scotland, 'The locals learned to buy and consume fresh vegetables with the arrival of Italian and Asian immigrants.' It was these communities who, following the customs of their countries, opened the first little fresh vegetable shops to supply fellow immigrants with the raw materials they craved to feel more at home. When I arrive at Eassie Farm, Sandy Pattullo, who started his crop over 30 years ago, confirms this idea, 'All we need are potatoes and turnips,' he remembers the distributors saying when they started trying to sell their asparagus. Today, good restaurants can't wait for the short season of these vegetables to start so that they can include them on the menu. He has sold the crop before even harvesting it.

I return to Edinburgh to catch my flight home. I have a few hours to spare and decide to visit the Scottish National Gallery. What was it that traditionally fed the country? I ask myself as I walk beneath the hundred-year-old paintings. About to return home, I feel like I have more questions than answers. I stop in front of an 1884 still life. It's by William York MacGregor, a Scottish painter. It is beautiful, with its quick brushstrokes and everything harmoniously thrown together on a wooden table and in wicker baskets: potatoes, turnips, leeks, cabbages, red cabbages, chard and rhubarb. A pair of stringed onions hang from a couple of hooks. Perhaps this is what the Scottish used to eat, I tell myself. It reflects what the climate allowed them to grow. I walk through the rooms, going back in time: in 1724 I find Richard Waitt, another Scottish painter. His painting is a still life with cauliflowers, birds and a leg of lamb. This doesn't surprise me, it's nothing that I haven't eaten during these days spent in Scotland. Looking at the dates of the paintings, this could well have been what Johnson and Boswell ate here as well. I'm not sure why, but this thought comforts me. Perhaps it's because I've just found an easy way to identify the culinary identity that I've been seeking. I can see a connection that hasn't been lost and, somehow, this satisfies me. I walk towards the exit with the feeling that these still lifes have provided an answer to my questions, and I'm still absorbed in these thoughts when, out of the corner of my eye, I see a familiar image. I turn around and move closer. Of course, I know it! An Old Woman Cooking Eggs, *1618, Velázquez.*

DUCK WITH FERMENTED HARICOT BEANS

Serves 8

COMPOSITION

—Mallard duck breast
—Fermented haricot beans
—Haricot bean *tempeto* purée
—Duck jus
—Foie gras in The Macallan Fine Oak 12 Years Old whisky
—Duck hollandaise sauce

FOR THE BRINE

2 kg water
200 g salt

Completely dissolve the salt in the cold water in a container. Refrigerate.

FOR THE MALLARD DUCK BREAST

2 mallard ducks
2 l brine (previously prepared)
Extra virgin olive oil

Using a knife, remove the breasts from the duck without separating them from the breast bone. Leave the skin on.

Set aside the remainder of the duck for later use.

Put the breasts with bone into a container and cover with the brine. After 40 minutes, take out the breasts and pat dry with kitchen paper.

Brown the breasts in a frying pan with extra virgin olive oil, starting on the bone side; then turn over and brown on all sides.

Once well browned, wrap the breasts in aluminium foil and leave to rest for about 5 minutes. Set aside.

FOR THE HARICOT BEAN *TEMPETO*

300 g dried haricot beans
1 l water (for soaking)
1 l water (for cooking)
1.5 g *Rhizopus Oryzae* fungus spores
10 Ziploc® bags
1 pin

Use the pin to prick small holes into both sides of the Ziploc® bags. Set aside until use.

Put the beans into a container with the water, cover and leave to soak in the refrigerator for at least 8 hours. Then discard the water and set aside the hydrated beans. Peel the beans by gently squeezing them out of their skins.

Combine the peeled beans in a stock pot with the water and bring to the boil. When it comes to the boil, cook over a medium heat for 15 minutes.

Next, spread the beans out over a tray and sprinkle with the fungus spores, stirring to ensure even distribution.

Put the beans into the perforated bags and leave to ferment at 30°C for 26 hours.

Then open the bags and remove the fermented beans. Set aside 50 g for the following step. Put the remainder of the beans into a bag and vacuum seal at 90% vacuum. Cook in a Roner at 50°C for 6 days. Then quickly cook in the bag in a blast chiller. Set aside.

FOR THE FERMENTED HARICOT BEANS

50 g fermented haricot beans (from preparing the haricot bean *tempeto*)

Cut the fermented beans into small dice.

FOR THE HARICOT BEAN *TEMPETO* PURÉE

150 g haricot bean *tempeto* (previously prepared)

Purée the *tempeto* with a hand-held blender. Press through a sieve and set aside in piping bags.

DUCK WITH FERMENTED HARICOT BEANS

FOR THE DUCK JUS

1 kg mallard duck meat and bones (from preparing the duck breast)
160 g onions
1.5 kg water
Extra virgin olive oil
Salt
0.4 g xanthan gum
10 g The Macallan Fine Oak 12 Years Old whisky
25 g haricot bean *tempeto* (previously prepared)

Cut up the duck into smaller pieces.

Cut the onions into julienne strips and brown in a frying pan. Put the bones and meat into a roasting tin and roast in the oven at 200°C until golden. Remove the excess fat and transfer to a stock pot with the browned onions and sauté well. Deglaze the caramelised juices in the roasting tin with a little water and add the liquid to the pot. Cover with cold water and cook over a low heat for 2 hours. Then strain into a container and leave to cool in the refrigerator.

When cold, scrape the fat from the surface and set aside. Transfer the jus to a pan over the heat and reduce to 200 g. Add the whisky at the last minute. Add the xanthan gum and use a hand-held blender to blend until thick. Then blend in 20 g of the previously removed fat and the 25 g of *tempeto*. Strain and set aside.

FOR THE FOIE GRAS MARINATED IN THE MACALLAN FINE OAK 12 YEARS OLD WHISKY

200 g foie gras
50 g sugar
50 g salt
20 g The Macallan Fine Oak 12 Years Old whisky

Mix the sugar, salt and whisky together in a bowl. Cut the foie gras into 1-cm-thick slices and coat completely in the whisky marinade. Marinate in the refrigerator for 1 hour.

Clean off the marinade and rinse with water, then purée the foie gras by pressing through a drum sieve. Set aside in a piping bag.

FOR THE BEURRE NOISETTE

1 kg unsalted butter

Heat the butter in a pan over a medium heat until it turns a light toasted colour and gives off an aroma similar to that of hazelnuts Strain and set aside.

FOR THE DUCK HOLLANDAISE SAUCE

140 g egg yolks
140 g duck jus (previously prepared)
420 g beurre noisette (previously prepared),
60 g walnut oil
Salt
Black peppercorns

Cook the egg yolks in a bowl in a bain-marie while stirring constantly with a whisk until their temperature reaches 65°C, without coagulating.

Whisk in the duck jus and remove from the heat, then add the beurre noisette and walnut oil and whisk to an emulsion. Season with salt and freshly ground pepper and set aside.

ASSEMBLY AND FINISHING

Samphire
Ice plant
Salt flakes

Remove the skin from the rested breasts. Cut the breast meat into thin slices and lightly heat.

Spread a teardrop of duck hollandaise sauce in the middle of a plate and cover with a tablespoon of duck jus. Arrange two slices of duck breast over the jus. Pipe five dots of haricot bean *tempeto* purée and two dots of foie gras marinated in The Macallan Fine Oak 12 Years Old whisky on the plate. Make two small mounds of fermented haricot beans around the duck breast. Garnish with the samphire, ice plant and a few salt flakes over the duck breast.

GROUSE HAGGIS

Serves 8

COMPOSITION

—Grouse sauce
—Grouse haggis
—Grouse fillets
—Grouse parfait
—Pumpkin purée
—Roasted pumpkin
—Sweet potato reduction

FOR THE MIREPOIX

1.5 kg onions
250 g carrots
150 g leeks
15 g extra virgin olive oil

Dice the vegetables into a mirepoix, put into a pan and cook in the oil over a low heat for 6 hours. Set aside.

FOR THE KUZU THICKENER

50 g kuzu *(Pueraria lobata)* starch
85 g cold water

Mix the ingredients together and set aside. Stir the preparation every time it is used.

FOR THE GROUSE SAUCE

1 kg red grouse* carcasses
120 g mirepoix (previously prepared)
2.5 kg water
15 g Pedro Ximénez
40 g kuzu thickener (previously prepared)

*The red grouse, *Lagopus lagopus scoticus*, is a species of wildfowl that is found on the Scottish moors during the hunting season.

Arrange the carcasses on a baking tray and roast them in the oven at 220°C. When golden, remove the excess fat and transfer to a stockpot. Deglaze the tray and add the juices to the pot. Add the mirepoix and cover the contents of the pot with very cold water.

Simmer for 3 hours over a very low heat, skimming constantly.

Strain and reduce to 250 g. Add the Pedro Ximénez and bring to the boil, then incorporate the kuzu starch while stirring constantly. Strain again and set aside.

FOR THE DUXELLES

120 g shallots
120 g white mushrooms
120 g porcini mushrooms *(Boletus edulis)*
30 g extra virgin olive oil
Salt

Finely chop all the ingredients. Sweat the shallots in the oil over a low heat. When soft, add the mushrooms and cook. Remove from the heat, season with salt and set aside.

FOR THE GROUSE HAGGIS

200 g foie gras
100 g milk
15 g armagnac
50 g egg whites
50 g white bread, crust removed
375 g red grouse meat
185 g pork dewlap
60 g foie gras
40 g truffle
90 g duxelles (previously prepared)
15 g salt

Cut the 200 g foie gras into 1.5-cm-wide strips and set aside.

Mix the milk with the armagnac and egg whites, then add the bread, soak for 15 minutes and blend.

Combine the grouse meat, pork dewlap, truffle and 60 g foie gras, and mince. Mix with the bread mixture, incorporate the forcemeat and season with salt.

Spread cling film on the work surface, add the mixture and roll tightly into a compact, 3-cm-diameter cylinder. Chill in a blast chiller. Vacuum seal in a bag and cook in a Roner at 63°C for 30 hours.

Then cool the cylinder and cut into 3-cm-long individual portions. Vacuum seal and set aside. Reheat before serving.

GROUSE HAGGIS

FOR THE GROUSE FILLETS
8 red grouse breasts

Vacuum seal the breasts in a bag and cook in a Roner at 63°C for 22 minutes. Cool quickly in a blast chiller and separate the fillets. Reserve the rest of the breasts for another use.

FOR THE GROUSE PARFAIT
1 kg red grouse livers
10 g extra virgin olive oil
10 g unsalted butter
150 g unsalted butter
Salt

Purge the livers of all blood by soaking in a bowl of iced water for 12 hours, changing the water every 3 hours. Wash well and drain.

In a frying pan with the olive oil and 10 g butter, brown the livers on both sides for 5 minutes. Transfer to a Thermomix with the remaining butter and blend at 70°C for 5 minutes. Set aside.

FOR THE PUMPKIN PURÉE
750 g pumpkin
150 g unsalted butter
50 g olive oil
Salt

Cut the pumpkin into pieces and roast over embers until cooked. Then peel and blend the flesh to a purée with the butter and oil. Season with salt and set aside in piping bags.

FOR THE ROASTED PUMPKIN
½ pumpkin
Salt

Cut the pumpkin vertically into 1.5-cm-thick slices. Season with salt and roast over embers.

FOR THE SWEET POTATO REDUCTION
2 kg sweet potatoes
600 g water
Extra virgin olive oil
Salt

Peel and wash the sweet potatoes. Cut into 1-cm-thick slices. In a frying pan with oil, sear the sweet potato slices on both sides until light golden. Add the water and bring to the boil. Reduce the heat to low and simmer for 30 minutes. Strain, pressing only lightly so as not to turn the liquid cloudy. Transfer the cooking liquid to a pan and reduce until intensely flavoured. Season with salt and set aside.

ASSEMBLY AND FINISHING
Place a slice of roasted pumpkin on a flat plate accompanied with a few dots of grouse parfait. Arrange a grouse fillet over the pumpkin and a grouse haggis disc next to it. Use a spoon to make small drop-shaped smears of pumpkin purée on the plate. Finally, cover the haggis with grouse sauce and drizzle the plate with sweet potato reduction.

FROZEN HONEY AND OAT MOUSSE

Serves 8

COMPOSITION
—Lemon granita
—Light carrot compote
—Honey parfait
—Caramelised oats

FOR THE LEMON GRANITA
1 kg lemon juice
100 g dextrose
100 g invert sugar
4 (2-g) gelatine leaves
Grated lemon zest

Heat part of the juice and dissolve the dextrose and invert sugar. While still hot, add the gelatine, filter through a fine-mesh sieve and incorporate the remaining ingredients. Fill 7-cm-wide and 25-cm-long half-cylinder silicone moulds and leave to set. Set aside.

FOR THE LIGHT CARROT COMPOTE
1 kg carrot purée
500 g sugar
11 g agar-agar

Heat the purée and dissolve the sugar. Add the agar-agar, blend and bring to the boil. Remove from the heat and blend again. Set aside.

FOR THE HONEY PARFAIT
150 g acacia honey
100 g pasteurised egg yolk
50 g water
100 g egg whites
100 g sugar
250 g cream
100 g lemon granita (previously prepared)

Combine the water, egg yolk and honey in a pan and heat to 85°C to pasteurise. Leave to cool and whip to a mousse-like consistency in a stand mixer.

Beat the egg whites with the sugar to stiff peaks.

Whip the cream.

Fold the three mixtures together, transfer to a piping bag, and fill a 17-cm-wide and 25-cm-long half-cylinder mould. Quickly insert the lemon granita core, cover with the honey parfait mixture, flatten the surface with a palette knife and freeze. Keep at -18°C until ready to serve.

FOR THE CARAMELISED OATS
100 g toasted oats
75 g sugar
50 g water

Combine the ingredients in a pan and bring to the boil while stirring constantly until the sugar caramelises and coats the oats. Leave to cool to room temperature. Set aside in an airtight container.

ASSEMBLY AND FINISHING
Bellflowers

Spread some carrot compote on a plate and add a piece of lemon granita-filled honey parfait. Arrange a line of caramelised oat 'rocks' over the parfait curve. Decorate with bellflowers.

RAZOR CLAMS WITH SEAWEED AND ANEMONES

Serves 8

COMPOSITION

—Razor clams
—Seaweed purée
—Seaweed and black garlic tartare
—Anemone sauce
—Seawater air

FOR THE BRINE

500 g water
50 g salt

Completely dissolve the salt in the cold water in a container. Set aside.

FOR THE RAZOR CLAMS

8 razor clams
Brine (previously prepared)

Wash the clams in a container of water. Soak in the brine for 10 minutes. Take out, rinse and drain off excess water. Vacuum seal the clams in a bag and cook in a Roner for 4 minutes at 63°C. Remove from the bag and take the meat out of the shells. Set aside the clams and the shells for the finishing stage.

FOR THE SEAWEED PURÉE

25 g basil leaves
60 g rocket leaves
30 g wakame *(Undaria pinnatifida)*
30 g sea lettuce *(Ulva lactuca)*
20 g water
½ clove garlic
50 g sunflower oil
1.5 g marine phytoplankton
Salt

Blanch the basil and rocket leaves in boiling salted water for 10 seconds and refresh immediately in an ice bath. Take out the leaves, draining off as much water as possible. Purée the leaves together with 20 g water, the garlic, wakame, sea lettuce and phytoplankton. Filter the purée through a drum sieve and use a hand-held blender to blend to an emulsion with the oil. Season with salt and set aside in a bain-marie.

FOR THE SEAWEED AND BLACK GARLIC TARTARE

30 g sea spaghetti *(Himanthalia elongata L.)*
20 g dulse *(Palmaria Palmata)*
10 g false Irish moss *(Mastocarpus stellatus)*
15 g black garlic purée

Wash the seaweed. Pat dry with kitchen paper. Finely chop the seaweed and mix with the black garlic purée. Set aside.

FOR THE ANEMONE SAUCE

300 g sea anemones
100 g extra virgin olive oil
85 g water
3 g salt
1 g sugar

Wash the anemones in a bowl of water and pat dry with kitchen paper.
In a frying pan with 20 g extra virgin olive oil, brown the anemones on both sides. Then deglaze the pan with the water and bring to the boil. Transfer the contents of the pan to a mixing beaker and blend using a hand-held blender to a very fine sauce. Strain, then blend to an emulsion with the remaining oil. Season with salt and sugar. Set aside.

FOR THE SEAWATER AIR

500 g bottled seawater
1 g soya lecithin

Mix the cold ingredients together and rest for at least 1 hour. Blend with a hand-held blender, frothing the surface well. Set aside.

ASSEMBLY AND FINISHING

Laurencia seaweed *(Laurencia sp.)*
Fennel shoots

Lightly reheat the clams and return them to their shells. Arrange each clam on a plate over a bed of anemone sauce. Alternate dots of seaweed purée and seaweed and black garlic tartare along the length of the clam. Decorate the top of each dot with fennel shoots and laurencia seaweed. Finally, add seawater air along one side of the razor clam.

OAT AND CHEDDAR BISCUIT

Serves 8

COMPOSITION
—Oat biscuit
—Cheddar cheese cream
—Deep-fried oats
—Sugar-coated oats

FOR THE OAT BISCUIT
30 g oat flour
60 g still mineral water
40 g milk
1 g salt

Combine all the ingredients in a non-stick frying pan and cook over a low heat for 5 minutes. Remove the pan from the heat and mix briskly until smooth. Pour the batter onto a silicone mat and give shape to the biscuits. Dry out in the dehydrator at 65°C for 3 hours.

FOR THE CHEDDAR CHEESE CREAM
100 g cheddar cheese
200 g milk
100 g cream (35% fat)
2 g soya lecithin
1 g xanthan gum
60 g unsalted butter

Chop up the cheese. Combine the cream and milk in a pan and bring to the boil. Remove the pan from the heat and add the lecithin and xanthan gum. Use a hand-held blender to blend until the xanthan gum has dissolved completely and the mixture thickens. While still hot, add the cheese and butter. Cover and leave to infuse for 10 minutes. Then blend again. Strain, fill a piping bag and set aside.

FOR THE COOKED OATS
100 g oat
1 kg water
4 g salt

Soak the oats in 250 g of water in a container for at least 12 hours in the refrigerator. Then drain and combine the oats with the remaining water in a pan. Bring to the boil and cook for about 20 minutes. Take out the cooked oats, drain off the excess water and dry. Set aside.

FOR THE DEEP-FRIED OATS
50 g cooked oats (previously prepared)
250 g sunflower oil
Salt

Spread the cooked oats over a silicone mat, spacing apart. Dry out in a dehydrator at 55°C for about 3 hours. Put the oil into a pan and heat to 210°C. Deep-fry the oats until light golden. Drain on kitchen paper and season with salt. Set aside.

FOR THE SUGAR-COATED OATS
50 g cooked oats (previously prepared)
25 g sugar
15 g water
Salt

Spread the cooked oats over a silicone mat, spacing apart. Dry out in a dehydrator at 55°C for about 1 hour 30 minutes. Remove and set aside.

Mix the water with the sugar in a pan and bring to the boil. Then add the oats and leave over the heat without allowing the oats to colour. As the water evaporates, the sugar will begin to crystallise. Then remove the pan from the heat and allow the water to continue to evaporate until all the oats develop a sugar coating. Season with salt and set aside.

ASSEMBLY AND FINISHING
Dandelion flowers

Pipe the cheddar cheese cream over the oat biscuits. Arrange sugar-coated and deep-fried oats over the cream. Decorate with dandelion petals.

WHITE ASPARAGUS WITH ELDERFLOWER AND ACACIA HONEY

Serves 8

COMPOSITION

—White asparagus ice cream
—Elderflower foam
—White asparagus tips
—White asparagus oil
—Cauliflower purée
—Dried apricots
—Acacia honey hollandaise sauce
—Bottarga

FOR THE WHITE ASPARAGUS ICE CREAM

570 g white asparagus spears
250 g cream (35% fat)
60 g skimmed milk powder
60 g dextrose
50 g food grade glycerine
7 g salt
5 g cream stabiliser

Peel the asparagus and cook until tender. Purée in a blender and filter through a fine-mesh conical sieve. Set aside.

Mix the cream, powdered milk and dextrose together in a pan and heat to 40°C.

Incorporate the glycerine and stabiliser. Use a hand-held blender to smooth away any lumps and pasteurise at 85°C. Add the salt, mix and leave to cool to 40°C. Finally, add the asparagus purée and blend until the mixture is smooth. Leave to mature in the refrigerator for 24 hours.

FOR THE ELDERFLOWER INFUSION

1 kg water
80 g sugar
40 g elderflowers

Heat the water with the sugar in a pan and add the elderflowers at 100°C. Remove from the heat and leave to infuse for 15 minutes. Strain, leave to cool and set aside.

FOR THE ELDERFLOWER FOAM

500 g elderflower infusion (previously prepared)
200 g egg whites
3 g xanthan gum
1½ gelatine leaves

Heat the infusion and thoroughly dissolve the softened gelatine. Add the rest of the ingredients and blend. Strain, fill a siphon and set aside.

FOR THE WHITE ASPARAGUS TIPS

32 white asparagus spears
1.6 g salt
0.3 g sugar

Peel the asparagus spears and cut off about 7 cm of the tips. Vacuum seal the tips in a bag with the salt and sugar, then cook in a Roner at 85°C for 30 minutes. Set aside the remainder of the asparagus spears to make the oil.

FOR THE WHITE ASPARAGUS OIL

100 g white asparagus spears (remainder after removing tips)
100 g sunflower oil
4 g salt

Go over the spears with a vegetable peeler or paring knife to remove any traces of skin that might have been left on when peeled. Rinse the spears in water, pat dry with kitchen paper, cut into mirepoix and put into a pan with the salt. Mix well and incorporate the oil. Place over a low heat and keep the oil at 70°C for 2 hours. Strain the oil and set aside.

FOR THE CAULIFLOWER PURÉE

1 kg cauliflower
100 g unsalted butter
Water
Salt

Bring salted water to the boil in a pan. Cut the cauliflower into florets of equal size. Blanch the cauliflower in the boiling water until tender. Drain well and blend to a very fine purée in a Thermomix. Add the butter and season with salt. Filter through a fine-mesh conical sieve and set aside.

FOR THE DRIED APRICOTS

2 dried apricots

Cut the dried apricots into 5-mm x 2-mm rectangles. Set aside.

WHITE ASPARAGUS WITH ELDERFLOWER AND ACACIA HONEY

FOR THE ACACIA HONEY HOLLANDAISE SAUCE
500 g unsalted butter
200 g egg yolks
75 g acacia honey

Heat the butter and clarify by allowing the butterfat to separate from the milk solids. Set aside the clarified butter.

Heat the egg yolk in a bowl over a bain-marie, beating constantly to prevent from coagulating, until the temperature reaches 85°C. Remove the bowl from the bain-marie and gradually incorporate the clarified butter. Finally, incorporate the honey. Fill a piping bag and set aside.

FOR THE BOTTARGA
100 g bottarga

Use a paring knife to peel the bottarga and cut into 2-mm-thick slices. Then cut the slices into 5-mm squares. Set aside.

ASSEMBLY AND FINISHING
Acacia honey
Tender almond kernel
Elderflowers
White miso paste

Keep the white asparagus tips hot. Place a tablespoon of cauliflower purée on a flat plate and arrange a quenelle of asparagus ice cream over it. Arrange 3 hot asparagus tips around and alternate with 3 dots of acacia honey hollandaise sauce, 3 dots of cauliflower purée and 3 dots of white miso paste. Position bottarga slices, dried apricot slices and the tender almond kernel on top of the dots. Cover the ice cream with the elderflower foam and finish the dish with elderflowers. Drizzle the white asparagus tips and foam with the white asparagus oil.

ROYAL HARE À LA ROYALE

Serves 8

COMPOSITION

—Royal hare quenelle
—Beetroot purée
—Earth air
—Hare sauce
—Hare civet
—Hare civet jus
—Smoked raspberry purée
—Hare cecina
—Royal hare liaison
—Hare loin

FOR THE DUXELLES

120 g white mushrooms
120 g porcini mushrooms
(Boletus edulis)
120 g shallots
30 g extra virgin olive oil

Clean and finely dice the mushrooms. Set aside. Peel and finely dice the shallots. Sweat in a frying pan with the oil until soft and lightly coloured. Add the mushrooms and allow the excess water to evaporate off. Then cook over a very low heat for 20 minutes. Set aside.

FOR THE ROYAL HARE

375 g hare meat
185 g pork dewlap
10 g black truffle
100 g hare livers
100 g milk
75 g hare blood
20 g armagnac
50 g pasteurised egg white
65 g white bread, crust removed
85 g duxelles (previously prepared)
12 g salt

Mince the hare meat with pork dewlap, truffle and livers.

Mix the milk with the blood, armagnac and egg whites, then add the bread, soak for 15 minutes and blend. Add with the duxelles to the minced mixture and season with salt.

Line a 4-cm deep and 12-cm square mould with cling film, smoothing out any wrinkles, and fill with 350 g of the royal hare mixture. Refrigerate for 1 hour. Put the mould inside a bag and vacuum seal at 100% vacuum. Cook in a Roner at 63°C for 30 hours, then cool quickly. Set aside.

FOR THE ROYAL HARE QUENELLE

500 g royal hare (previously prepared)

Use a fork to lightly crush the royal hare. Use two spoons to make quenelles weighing about 4 g each. Set aside.

FOR THE EARTH DISTILLATE

300 g soil
500 g water

Mix the ingredients together in a container, cover with a lid and leave to infuse in the refrigerator for 12 hours.

Pour the infusion into the evaporation flask, with a 0.22-µm membrane filter positioned between the flask and the outlet towards the condenser.

Distil the earth at 30–35°C (bath temperature) for 1–2 hours and finish at 40–45°C for 30 minutes.

Vacuum seal the distillate to prevent loss of aroma. If the distillate is to be stored for several days or weeks, it should be frozen.

ROYAL HARE À LA ROYALE

FOR THE BEETROOT PURÉE
150 g beetroot
25 g earth distillate (previously prepared)
0.2 g xanthan gum
Salt

Boil the beetroot until tender. Blend with the earth distillate and xanthan gum, then filter through a fine conical sieve. Season with salt, fill a squeeze bottle and set aside.

FOR THE EARTH AIR
250 g earth distillate (previously prepared)
1.5 g sucroester
3.5 g soya lecithin

Combine all the ingredients, mix well and rest. Blend with a hand-held blender, frothing well. Set aside.

FOR THE MIREPOIX
1.3 kg onions
200 g carrots
175 g leeks
20 g extra virgin olive oil

Dice the vegetables into a mirepoix, put into a pan and cook in the oil over a low heat for 6 hours. Set aside.

FOR THE HARE JUS
850 g hare bones
200 g mirepoix (previously prepared)
75 g red wine
1.5 kg very cold water

Put the bones into a roasting tin and roast in the oven at 180°C. When golden, remove the excess fat and transfer to a stockpot. Deglaze the tray to dissolve the caramelised juices and add to the pot with the bones. Add the mirepoix and wine, bring to the boil and cover with the water.

Bring to the boil, skim off the scum and cook over a very low heat for 3 hours. Then strain and reduce the liquid to make 200 g of hare jus. Leave to cool and set aside.

FOR THE KUZU THICKENER
150 g kuzu *(Pueraria lobata)* starch
250 g cold water

Mix the ingredients together and set aside. Stir the preparation every time it is used.

FOR THE HARE SAUCE
200 g hare jus (previously prepared)
20 g kuzu thickener (previously prepared)
30 g unsalted butter
40 g hare blood

Heat the hare jus and add the kuzu thickener and butter while whisking briskly to make a stable emulsion free of lumps. Strain. Immediately before serving, stir in the hare blood to a smooth and fine sauce.

FOR THE LARD
50 g pork belly fat
5 g water
25 g sunflower oil

Cut the fat into 1-cm cubes, using as much of the fat as possible. Put the fat into a pan with the water and oil. Cook over a low heat until all the water has evaporated and as much of the fat as possible has melted. Strain, leave to cool and set aside.

ROYAL HARE À LA ROYALE

FOR THE HARE CIVET

4 (200-g) hare shoulders
150 g leeks
150 g carrots
75 g celery
250 g onions
½ bay leaf
2 sprigs thyme
2 sprigs rosemary
½ stick cinnamon
5 g black peppercorns
3 g juniper berries
Peel of ½ lemon
Peel of ½ orange
1 l red wine
60 g lard (previously prepared)
Olive oil

Peel and dice the vegetables into a mirepoix. Combine all the ingredients, except the lard and oil, in an airtight container and marinate for 24 hours. Then remove the shoulders and clean off all traces of the marinade. Lightly sear in a frying pan with a little olive oil. Leave to cool and set aside.

Strain the marinade liquid and reduce to a third in a pan, skimming constantly. Set aside.

Separate out all the aromatics from the marinade (juniper berries, cinnamon stick, peppercorns, orange and lemon peel, thyme, rosemary and bay leaf) and set aside.

Put the mirepoix from the marinade into a pan and sauté until they have lost all their liquid and turn soft. Cool quickly and set aside.

Combine 2 hare shoulders with 50 g sautéed mirepoix, 30 g lard and 100 g marinade reduction into 2 bags and vacuum seal. Cook sous-vide in a Roner at 63°C for 24 hours. Then open the bags and filter the cooking liquid through a fine conical strainer. Leave to cool and remove any excess fat. Set aside.

Bone the hare shoulders, leaving the pieces of meat as large as possible.

FOR THE HARE CIVET JUS

200 g hare shoulder cooking liquid (from preparing the hare civet)
133 g marinade reduction (from preparing the hare civet)
10 g sugar
Herbs, spices and citrus peel (from preparing the hare civet)
40 g kuzu thickener (previously prepared)

Bring the hare shoulder cooking liquid to the boil in a pan and skim.

Incorporate the marinade liquid reduction and sugar, bring back to the boil and skim. Take the pan off the heat and add the aromatics. Cover and leave to infuse for 30 minutes. Strain and thicken with the kuzu thickener, then strain again and set aside.

FOR THE SMOKED RASPBERRY PURÉE

250 g raspberries
10 g extra virgin olive oil

Put the raspberries in a fine-mesh drum sieve. Put glowing embers into another container and place the sieve with the strawberries over them. Drizzle with a little oil. Cover quickly with cling film and leave to smoke for 5 minutes. Then take out the raspberries, purée and filter through a fine conical sieve. Set aside.

FOR THE SPICE MIXTURE

10 g ground cloves
30 g sweet paprika
40 g Cabernet Sauvignon red wine vinegar

Mix the ingredients together in a container, cover with a lid and rest in the refrigerator for 24 hours.

ROYAL HARE À LA ROYALE

FOR THE HARE CECINA

2 (200-g) hare shoulders
1 kg coarse salt
350 g sugar
0.3 g curing salt (sodium nitrate)
80 g spice mixture (previously prepared)
Smoker
Holm oak embers

Put the shoulders into a container with ice and water and soak for 24 hours to purge of blood. Change the water every 6 hours.

Dry the shoulders and transfer to another container. Cover with the coarse salt, sugar and curing salt. Refrigerate for 24 hours.

Then clean the shoulders well and brush with the spice mixture. Hang them in the smoker with holm oak embers until they lose 5% of their water (3–4 days).

Take the shoulders out of the smoker and hang in a cool and dry place for 1 ½ weeks.

Vacuum seal the hare cecina with 100% vacuum and set aside until use.

FOR THE HARE LIVER PÂTÉ

110 g hare livers
110 g unsalted butter
10 g extra virgin olive oil
Salt

Soak the livers in an ice bath for 12 hours to purge of any blood. Then take them out and dry well.

Heat the oil in a frying pan and sauté the livers until cooked through. Blend together with the butter and season with salt. Press through a fine-mesh drum sieve, leave to cool and set aside.

FOR THE ROYAL HARE LIAISON

130 g hare jus (previously prepared)
40 g egg
15 g hare liver pâté (previously prepared)
Salt

Use a hand-held blender to blend the ingredients together and season with salt. Put 40 g of the mixture onto each of 8 deep plates and wrap in cling film. Cook in a steam oven at 90°C for 10 minutes and set aside.

FOR THE HARE LOIN

2 hare loins
Extra virgin olive oil
Salt

Season the loins with salt and sear on a griddle. Set aside.

ASSEMBLY AND FINISHING

Cocoa powder
Beetroot shoots
Ground juniper berries
Hazelnuts

Reheat the plates containing the royal hare liaison in a steam oven at 65°C for about 7 minutes. Then remove the cling film and pour a tablespoon of hare sauce over the liaison. Alternate dots of beetroot purée and smoked raspberry purée along the edge of the liaison.

Heat the civet in the civet jus and place a small amount over the centre of the royal hare liaison. Sprinkle with cocoa powder and ground juniper berries. Place a very hot royal hare quenelle next to the civet and arrange a slice of seared hare loin next to it.

Finish the dish with a few beetroot shoots over the beetroot purée and a few broken hazelnut pieces. Sprinkle with freshly grated hare cecina and put a little earth air in a line with the meat on the plate.

OAT CURD CREAM AND CARAMEL

Serves 8

COMPOSITION

—Oat curd cream
—Caramel jelly
—Oat caramel

FOR THE OAT CURD CREAM

500 g cream
500 g milk
100 g toasted oats
75 g sugar
7 g iota carrageenan

Combine the milk and cream in a pan and bring to the boil. Add the oats, quickly take off the heat and steep for 10 minutes. Strain, return to the pan and add the iota carrageenan mixed with the sugar. Return the pan to the heat and bring to the boil while stirring constantly. Remove from the heat and put four tablespoons of the cream into each plate. Leave to set in the refrigerator.

FOR THE CARAMEL JELLY

200 g water
100 g sugar
1.5 g agar-agar

Mix the sugar with the agar-agar in a pan. Add the cold water and bring to the boil while stirring constantly. Leave to cool a little, then cover the cream with a fine layer of jelly.

FOR THE OAT CARAMEL

200 g sugar
100 g isomalt
100 g glucose
100 g water
20 g oat powder
20 g toasted oats

Combine the sugars in a pan and bring to the boil, avoid stirring to prevent from crystallising. Heat to 160°C, then lower the temperature to 140°C and add the oat powder. Leave to cool.

Grind the cold caramel into a very fine powder and set aside. Use a sieve to sprinkle the powder over a silicone mat, arrange a few oats over it and bake at 180°C until the caramel turns clear.

Set aside in an airtight container with silica gel until use.

ASSEMBLY AND FINISHING

Serve the cold cream with a caramel sheet on the edge of the plate. The caramel is broken and eaten with the cream to add crunch.

HUNTLY
SPEYSIDE
ABERDEEN
ARBROATH

EAST COAST

Josep on the banks of the River Spey at The Macallan Distillery. Previous page: Auchmitie Beach, near Arbroath

‘It is in truth not for glory, nor riches, nor honours that we are fighting, but for freedom – for that alone, which no honest man gives up but with life itself.’ Arbroath Abbey, 1320.

The Scottish nobles sent this letter to Pope John XXII asking for the recognition of an independent Scotland. Also, they asked for the lifting of the excommunication of Robert Bruce, a man they saw as their king. Since Alexander III of Scotland had died without an heir in 1286, England had been trying to annex Scotland, with successive invasions. The Avignon Pope, who had intervened, permitting Edward II of England’s raids into Scotland, took the Arbroath declaration into consideration, but couldn’t persuade the English to give up. The Catholic Church wanted a truce in the hostilities, but this wasn’t achieved until 1328 when the Treaty of Northampton was signed, and it was short-lived. Through this treaty, England, in the midst of a political crisis following the king’s assassination, acknowledged Scotland’s independence and Bruce as king.

This letter, which was sent from Robert Bruce’s chancery located in the abbey, has often been considered to be the first formal declaration of independence reflecting the will of the people. However, others see the message as an example of using supposed popular will to serve the interests of the nobles.

What, in its day, was one of the most important Benedictine landmarks in the country had already fallen into ruin by the time Johnson and Boswell arrived in Arbroath. Its decline started in 1561 with the arrival of the Protestant Reformation in Scotland. However, its historical and symbolic value is well known, and when Johnson and Boswell visited the ruins that were overgrown with weeds only a few stones were left, as a result of people using the stones from the abbey to build other buildings in the town.

Josep, Arbroath

It's both challenging and audacious attempting to extract the essence of a country that is not one's own. Although I believe it's not comparable with the responsibility that would come with doing so with my own country. Some might say that the perspective of a foreigner strips away prejudices and guarantees a degree of impartiality. However, it's not necessarily the case: all stories first pass through the storyteller's filter and then that of the listener. For this reason, I like the idea of distilling Scotland, as Joan has written in his notes, as if the way to obtain the essence were a question of physics rather than of human passions and opinions.

The ruins of Arbroath Abbey are made of red sandstone, just like the cliffs that plunge into the North Sea. Still standing and two-dimensional like a theatre backdrop, you can see part of the main façade. Above this, there is a floating circular hole that formerly housed a rose window. Behind are the plinths, which had once supported the major columns, and make two lines leading to the altar. There are no vaults in existence: above is the sky, below, a carpet of grass and level with the high altar is an austere tombstone with a short inscription: 'William The Lion. King of Scots', in honour of the man who founded the abbey. As Dr Johnson wrote, just contemplating the ruins provides an idea of its 'ancient magnificence'.[1] Between these dilapidated walls I walk the shape of the Latin cross that can still be made out on the ground. I walk in the footsteps of Johnson and Boswell, along the same ways that have been travelled by others throughout history. I do so with the hope of ensuring that these pathways, opened up with the persistence of walkers, don't once again get covered by weeds.

---

1 Johnson, S. (1984). *A Journey to the Western Islands of Scotland*. London: Penguin Classics.

‘I LIKE THE IDEA OF DISTILLING SCOTLAND, AS JOAN HAS WRITTEN IN HIS NOTES, AS IF THE WAY TO OBTAIN THE ESSENCE WERE A QUESTION OF PHYSICS RATHER THAN OF HUMAN PASSIONS AND OPINIONS.’

—JOSEP ROCA

There are times in which metaphors lose their figurative meaning and once again become literal. Something like this happens with Arbroath Abbey, from which the light, projected from inside through the rose window, became not only a spiritual guide for faithful Christians, but also a lighthouse to guide mariners' boats along the Scottish coast. Scotland comes and goes by the sea. The sea has always been one more infrastructure in its communication network. And this, somehow, turns it into land. In the same way, perhaps, that the fine network of lakes, rivers and bodies of water running over its surface turns part of its land into water. This hybrid geography provokes two simultaneous phenomena: that Scots live with their backs to both the sea and the land. Or, perhaps they face both, but without specifically valuing what it means to have one thing when they have everything.

ARBROATH SMOKIES

The area of Arbroath is the land of smoked fish. Although today the product is associated with the town to such an extent that it's difficult to say its name without thinking of the food, Arbroath's relationship with smoked haddock is fairly recent, dating from the nineteenth century. Until then, it was Auchmithie, a tiny fishing village a few kilometres north, where the fish were traditionally preserved with smoke. Although the origin of the technique in Scotland is not certain, because of the similarity with the Scandinavian technique, it is probable that it was the Vikings who introduced this art in the early eleventh century.

The streets of Arbroath run from the abbey, at the top of the town, towards the port. The smokeries form part of the character of the place. Josep and Eric Oliu, the head waiter at El Celler who has joined him for the trip, meet Iain R. Spink, one of the producers who has most promoted smokies both nationally and internationally. They've arranged to meet him on the coast at Auchmithie, probably the most symbolic place to witness this ritual. 'Where there's smoke, there's fire': although they hadn't arranged a specific spot to meet Iain, it's not difficult to find him. The scene really is photo-worthy: Iain is getting a fire going in an old whisky barrel beneath a cliff, on a level area of land, right next to the sea. On one side, there are two easels supporting six sticks between them. The haddocks, joined at the tail with a piece of string, hang over the stick waiting to enter the essential tool: the smoker.

When the fire is really going, the show begins. Iain works precisely, moving with ease among his equipment. In the blink of an eye, the sticks are supported on the edges of the barrel and the haddocks hang at the optimum distance

IAIN IS GETTING A FIRE GOING IN AN OLD WHISKY BARREL BENEATH A CLIFF, ON A LEVEL AREA OF LAND, RIGHT NEXT TO THE SEA. ON ONE SIDE, THERE ARE TWO EASELS SUPPORTING SIX STICKS BETWEEN THEM. THE HADDOCKS, JOINED AT THE TAIL WITH A PIECE OF STRING, HANG OVER THE STICK WAITING TO ENTER THE ESSENTIAL TOOL: THE SMOKER.

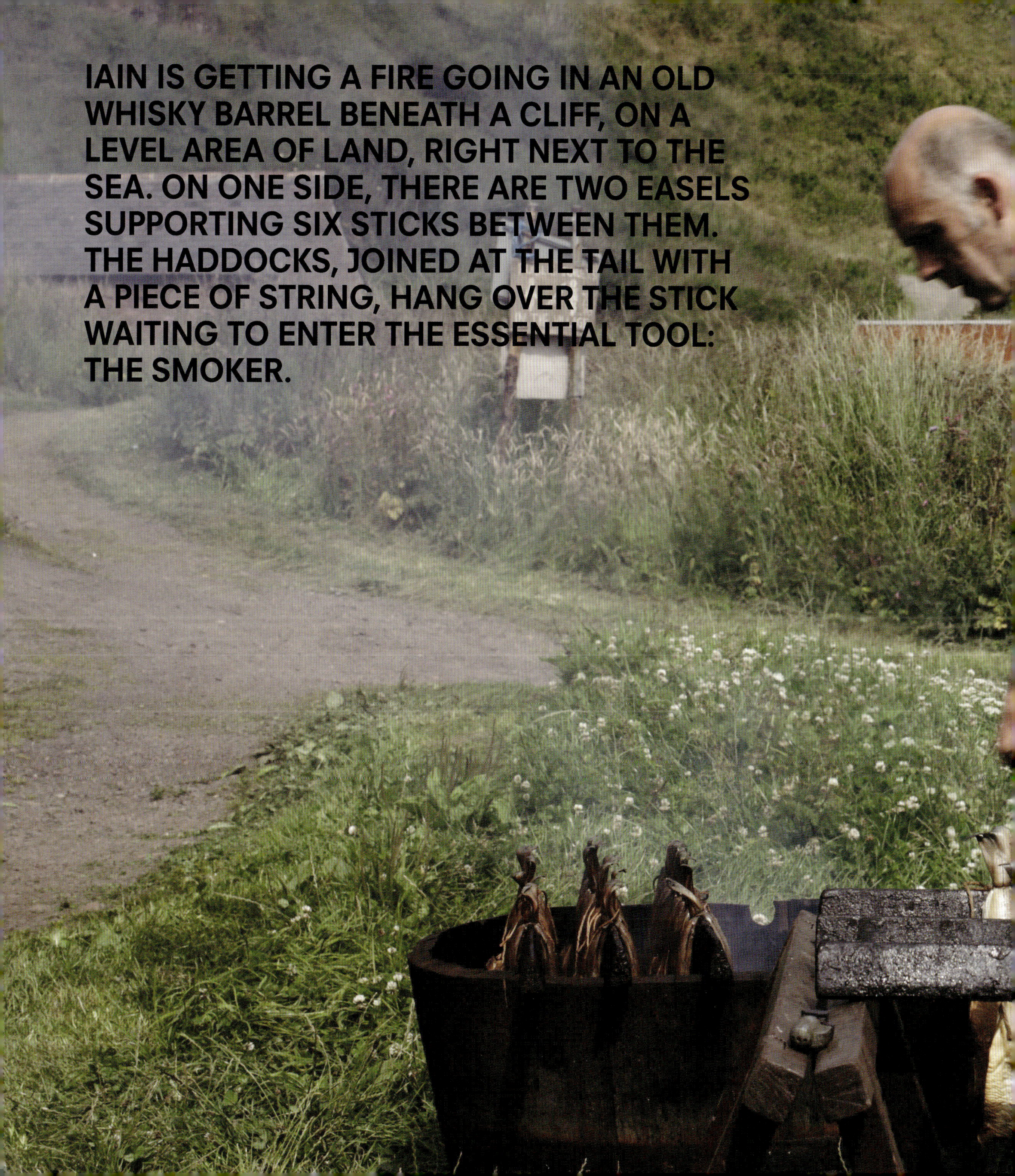

from the fire. He covers the barrel with damp hessian and leaves them for the 40 minutes, approximately, that they will need to smoke. Meanwhile, he explains the ins and outs of the process to his guests: 'I buy the fish at the morning market. I'm not a fisherman, I don't like going out to sea. I scale and clean them, then I leave them to mature in salt — with one layer of salt, one of fish, another of salt, etc. — for a couple of hours, depending on their size and consistency. Next, I wash them, tie them together in pairs and hang them to air for a short while.' Carrying out this process outdoors while it's raining doesn't cause any problems: it's just slower. However, it is harder to control when there is too much wind as this fans the flames and the times speed up. The process that takes place inside the barrel has two parts: smoking and cooking. This means that the haddock can be eaten straight out of the barrel. 'Any fish can be used, as long as it isn't hung for too long. I've tried it with mackerel, herring and sole as these were the fish that the fishwives traditionally smoked. Traditionally, the women smoked the fish that their husbands fished,' tells Iain while he shows Josep and Eric a book of photographs from the nineteenth century documenting the process.

He works without any apparent temperature control, but with a wealth of experience and the genetics of five generations of fish smokers. It is a lesson for me. Iain is full of passion, it's clear that he's crazy about what he does. He tells us that his father fought for Arbroath smokies to get the recognition they deserve for their quality, connection with the land and the know-how accumulated by the people who make them. It's because of this that today they're protected by a designation of origin. We try the first haddock straight out of the barrel. Iain opens the two fillets. The colour and shape of the fillet that comes away from the bone reveal that it is cooked to perfection. It really is something very special! The outside

Previous page: Iain R. Spink, maker of Arbroath Smokies

of the fish has a nice smoked flavour, while inside it is juicy and you can taste the fish flavour: it's an exquisite combination. With a product of this quality, I'm not surprised that, at the fairs and markets where it is sold, people have swapped their hamburgers and hot dogs for smoked haddock. He says that it's because the work they do is very visual; it's a 'demonstration of craftsmanship'. He's right: the work he does is very aesthetic, but if it were just this, his customers would just watch, as spectators. I'm convinced, after trying them, that the reason why people come up to his smokies stall is to eat them.

Still enveloped in the aromas of oak and beech, Iain's two favourite types of wood for smoking his fish, the travellers stop off at nearby Gordon's Restaurant, before continuing their journey. Garry Watson, the chef and owner, greets them as they enter. Smokies are one of his favourite products, so they feature in the conversation and on the menu, in which he serves them with a cauliflower velouté soup. Gordon's is one of those reliable, traditional restaurants where you find good local products prepared in a classic way. 'I'm influenced, through my dad, by French cooking. I like to keep things simple by cooking with local products in a respectful way, the menu writes itself,' says Garry.

The east coast sections of Johnson and Boswell's trip passed by quickly. It seems as though, with their aim of reaching the Highlands and Western Isles, this part of Scotland didn't interest them so much. Although they made the trip together, their books diverged from the very beginning. Johnson's age and learning made his tale a historical, anthropological and philosophical document. Boswell also included these aspects, but did so more informally, and his book is a source of endless anecdotes. His admiration of Johnson

‘WE TRY THE FIRST HADDOCK STRAIGHT OUT OF THE BARREL. IAIN OPENS THE TWO FILLETS. THE COLOUR AND SHAPE OF THE FILLET THAT COMES AWAY FROM THE BONE REVEAL THAT IT IS COOKED TO PERFECTION. IT REALLY IS SOMETHING VERY SPECIAL! THE OUTSIDE OF THE FISH HAS A NICE SMOKED FLAVOUR, WHILE INSIDE IT IS JUICY AND YOU CAN TASTE THE FISH FLAVOUR: IT’S AN EXQUISITE COMBINATION.’

—JOSEP ROCA

— both as a person and literary speaking — is clear; perhaps without realising it he was already writing his friend's biography. For example, Boswell notes how Johnson called the waiter of a sorry inn they stayed at in Montrose 'Rascal!'[2] when he stirred a lump of sugar into Johnson's lemonade using his finger. The doctor was an honourable, formal man with elegant manners. He wanted to retain his good reputation and wasn't prepared to forgo his English manners, even though at times the circumstances may have required it. 'Sir, it is very bad manners to carry provisions to any man's house, as if he could not entertain you. To an inferior, it is oppressive; to a superior, it is insolent,'[3] is how he replied to Boswell's suggestion of taking lemons with them to make sure that he could drink lemonade throughout the journey.

---

2 Boswell, J. (1807). *The Journal of a Tour to the Hebrides*. London: T. Cadwell and W. Davies.

3 Ibid.

LAND OF UNDERRATED VEGETABLES

The writers' tales aren't specifically about cuisine, but they inevitably include details about the products they see and eat. Describing one of the meals they eat in Aberdeen, Boswell writes, 'At dinner, Dr Johnson ate several platefuls of Scotch broth, with barley and peas in it, and seemed very fond of the dish.'[4] This, and other examples, provide a broad depiction of what was eaten in Scotland in the late eighteenth century. Or, to be more precise, what was eaten in Scotland by those with means, as this was the sector of society that the protagonists rubbed shoulders with. However, Johnson and Boswell also record the customs of the humbler people that they meet along the way. For example, one constant is the limited use of fresh vegetables. The peas found in Scotch broth soup are dried. Also, the ingredients that add flavour to this soup — usually made with the lesser-valued cuts of lamb — are turnip, carrot, leek, cabbage and celery. These vegetables are the five pillars of common soups, in Scotland, as well as in cooler and warmer parts of Europe.

The further north you travel, the shorter the vegetable season and the harsher the vegetable-growing conditions. Josep and Eric visit Vital Veg in Inverurie. In these fields some of the vegetables that supply the local markets are grown, following a crop rotation system split into five plots of land. The manager, Wendy Seel, guides her visitors through the different areas and explains the advantages of the method they use. The vegetables are divided up into families, depending on their relationship with the soil: namely, how deep their roots grow and what type of nutrients they absorb. This way of grouping them

4 Boswell, J. (1807). *The Journal of a Tour to the Hebrides*. London: T. Cadwell and W. Davies.

Josep with Wendy Seel of Vital Veg

VITAL VEG

allows a certain balance to be kept in the plot of land and creates beneficial relationships, from one harvest to the next, between the vegetable families that rotate.

'The growing conditions here are harsh, we can have snow until April and the season ends in September,' says Wendy. 'Also, as a producer, you want everything: a winter that is cold enough to kill pests, but not so cold that it finishes off the cauliflowers,' she continues, while they approach the brassicas plot. Here, with a smile, she recites the long list of all the types of cabbage they grow. 'Yes, it's the plant that grows best here. It's not the most attractive plant, but our customers are learning to appreciate it. It's an underrated vegetable,' she says, appearing to excuse the abundance of this crop. With the aim of protecting the more delicate plants from the cold winds, Vital Veg is surrounded by a protective belt of trees and bushes that also produce fruits. The three species forming this shield are mountain ash, elderflower and crab apple trees. The first two provide berries and the third, a small bitter fruit. They can all be used to make jams or jellies.

A CUISINE ABOUT TO FLOURISH

Johnson and Boswell's trip raised expectations amongst the locals as they progressed. Many had heard of the doctor who had arrived from England and the route he was taking through the country, so they were pleased when the pair chose to stop in their towns. There were some that got the wrong end of the stick, which caused funny anecdotes, like the one that Boswell recounts of a conversation over breakfast at a house they stayed at in Ellon:

'The landlady said to me, "Is not this the great doctor that is going about through the country?"

I said, "Yes."

"Ay," said she, "We heard of him, I made an errand into the room on purpose to see him. There's something great in his appearance: it is a pleasure to have such a man in one's house; a man who does so much good. If I had thought of it, I would have shown him a child of mine, who has had a lump on his throat for some time."

"But," said I, "he is not a doctor of physique [...] he is only a very learned man. They say he is the greatest man in England, except Lord Mansfield."'[5]

Although today, Scotland, like many other places, is a country that attracts a lot of tourists, not many would cite Scottish cuisine as the main reason

5 Boswell, J. (1807). *The Journal of a Tour to the Hebrides*. London: T. Cadwell and W. Davies.

behind their trip. However, the idea that it has the most vibrant cuisine in the United Kingdom is starting to gain ground. Despite this, a visit from the Roca brothers, who want to witness this movement, is often met with pleasant surprise.

> *They have a great, plentiful larder and, although the recognition from a foreigner like me fills them with pride, sometimes I see a degree of surprise when they receive the praise. It's as if they themselves don't believe it or don't sufficiently value what they have. Personally, I believe that everything is set for their cuisine to flourish: there is an excellent product, an extremely beautiful natural environment, tourism that is becoming increasingly established and economic stability. So, perhaps the only thing that is missing is leadership, someone who is ready to take on this role, from a restaurant, for example.*

A COUNTRY'S IDENTITY: SHORTBREAD AND WHISKY

Instead of following the route along the coast, Josep and Eric continue inland, leaving the footsteps of the writers for a while, in a pattern that is repeated throughout the journey. This is sometimes due to the different aims of the travellers and sometimes because of improvements to the infrastructure that have been made over the two and a half centuries that separate the trips. There are few products that truly identify a country in a foreigner's mind. And not many would disagree with the fact that for Scotland, two of these products are whisky and shortbread. Going in search of these is, therefore, reason enough for the next stop: Dean's of Huntly. Here, Bill Dean welcomes his visitors to the workshop where they make buttery shortbread, amongst other specialities. 'The butter is important. For quality reasons we only buy it from four suppliers with whom we feel comfortable working,' explains Bill. There are few other secrets behind the success of this business that produces 17 million portions a year. A business that began because of how well Bill's wife Helen's biscuits were received amongst friends. 'We bake the shortbread for an hour and a half at 150°C, a lower temperature than usual; this is why the process takes longer. Also, we don't use moulds to prick the surface, we continue to use a more traditional technique using a fork. It takes us five hours to get a finished product, while this process, when completely industrialised, can be reduced to an hour,' he adds, hazarding reasons for why the quality of the shortbread is so renowned.

Bill Dean of Dean's of Huntly
On the right: Freshly baked shortbread

The two most common shortbread formats are the fingers, and the rounds that are cut into eight pieces, called petticoat tails. The origin of this name, although not certain, could be the petticoats of the women in Mary, Queen of Scots' court in the sixteenth century and their fondness for this biscuit which, originally — as far back as the twelfth century — was flavoured with caraway.

> *I feel connected to Scotland by some emotional links: while here I've observed and felt a cultural and political twinning with my home, Catalonia. There are also professional and affective connections and whisky is one of these, I can't help but get excited about its complex simplicity. A nation is made out of what it eats, but also, what it drinks, and whisky is Scotland's national drink. A drink that is made from the pure water of its rivers, barley, peat and the age-old knowledge of how to transform these ingredients. They are the essential elements of a landscape and the characteristics of its people converted into a drink. The features of a drink to reflect, in its likeness, the character of a community. It's a mutual construction of identity. Whiskies such as The Macallan Single Malt also connect the two countries of Scotland and Spain through the poetic journey of its exceptional oak casks. The individual staves that unite, form the shape of the cask and are hand-crafted, toasted to flavor and finally filled with sherry. This time aged process all takes place in Jerez, and it is from that same place that the casks — once the liquid has been removed — begin their journey to The Macallan's spiritual home in Speyside. This noble oak wood from northern Spain, dried and soaked with sherry from the south, determines the signature flavor of The Macallan.*

Thanks to our friendship with The Macallan, El Celler has a barrel of whisky ageing at the Speyside distillery next to the River Spey, which is where the water is sourced from to create this peerless spirit. The investment in the exceptional oak casks ensures they can make the long journey across Spain before reaching the distillery on Speyside; however, for our cask there was an additional stop in Girona. There, we emptied and bottled the 136 litres of Palo Cortado sherry, which were used to mark the 30th anniversary of El Celler. Once emptied, the barrel travelled to The Macallan distillery, where 30 litres of a 30-year-old whisky were barrelled to age for three months. This whisky was then bottled and lastly the barrel was again filled with a whisky, which is now in its second year and will be aged for 12 years.

It is therefore whisky and friendship that brings Josep to the banks of the River Spey, an important source of salmon in the area, to meet Ken Grier, the former Creative Director for The Macallan. About the Roca brothers he says, 'We love collaborating with such lovely, brilliant people and they are both of these things.' Fully aware of the reason why Josep is there, Ken has organised a special family style meal: more than twenty traditional Scottish dishes, some of which are recipes that have existed for hundreds of years. The room's grand table is laden with creations, showcasing a culinary feast: there are bannocks,[6] Scotch pies,[7] Scotch eggs, fish and chips and cullen skink.[8] They taste Angus-breed oxtail, lamb, venison and game sausages. There are both cheese and potato scones and many different varieties of

---

6 Unleavened bread, originally made from barley or oat flour.

7 A meat pie made with minced mutton and vegetables.

8 A fish soup flavoured with smoked haddock bones and finished with milk and/or cream.

local cheese. The conversations about what they eat allow more dishes to arrive onto the already overloaded table. The banquet is extended with other recipes and descriptions of what they haven't eaten. Then, it finishes with some of the most traditional desserts: Empire biscuits,[9] Victoria sponge,[10] cranachan[11] and clootie dumpling.[12] Josep has left Johnson and Boswell's route to visit his friend. On the other hand, on the table he has found a good selection of the recipes that the writers may have eaten in 1773.

---

9 A layer of jam in between two shortbread biscuits, covered with white icing and finished with a glacé cherry.

10 A sponge cake filled with buttercream and jam, often eaten at weddings.

11 Made with oats, cream, whisky and raspberries.

12 A type of pudding made with spices and dried fruit. It is wrapped in a floured cloth and steamed, where the name comes from (clootie is the old English word for cloth).

On the right: Scotch pies. Empire biscuits. Stovies roast beef potatoes. Victoria sponge. Scones. Cullen skink. Scotch eggs. Bannocks

Stovies
Roast Beef Potatoes

Josep and Ken Grier, former Creative Director of The Macallan

PARTRIDGE WITH CABBAGE

Serves 8

COMPOSITION

—Partridge breast
—Pan-fried fermented cabbage juice
—Green cabbage ravioli
—Cabbage and tarragon foam
—Romanesco
—Kale crisp
—Kale juice
—Cauliflower florets
—White cabbage couscous
—Red arrow broccoli florets
—Broccoli buds

FOR THE BRINE

1 kg water
100 g salt

Completely dissolve the salt in the cold water. Set aside.

FOR THE PARTRIDGE BREAST

4 partridges
Brine (previously prepared)
Black peppercorns

Clean the partridges, cut out the breasts and set aside the remaining meat. Soak the breasts in the brine for 8 minutes. Drain and pat dry with kitchen paper.

Sear the breasts on both sides in a frying pan with olive oil over a high heat. Take them out of the pan, season with freshly ground pepper and rest. Set aside and keep hot until ready to serve.

FOR THE PARTRIDGE STOCK

2 kg partridge bones and legs (leftover from preparing the breasts)
100 g extra virgin olive oil
200 g onion
3 kg water

In a frying pan with the olive oil, lightly sear the bones and legs, then remove from the pan. Cut the onion into julienne strips and sweat in the same pan until translucent. Return the bones and legs to the pan with the water and bring to the boil. When the water comes to the boil, turn the heat down to low and leave to reduce at a simmer for about 1 hour. Strain and set the stock aside.

FOR THE BACON STOCK

200 g smoked bacon
300 g water
Xanthan gum

Cut the bacon into 2-cm cubes. Vacuum seal in a bag with the water and cook in a Roner at 85°C for 2 hours. Then open the bag and strain the liquid. Set aside both the stock and meat.

Thicken the stock with the xanthan gum, dissolving completely. Use 0.3 g of xanthan gum for every 100 g of stock.

FOR THE FERMENTED CABBAGE

1.5 kg white cabbage
50 g salt

Remove the outer leaves and wash the cabbage. Cut into julienne strips. In a container, mix the cabbage with the salt and squeeze until you see that water is released. Cover with cling film and place a weight on top so that the cabbage is covered with liquid. Leave to ferment at 18–20°C for 4 days. Then continue the fermentation process in the refrigerator at 3°C for 3 more days. Finally, vacuum seal in a bag and set aside in the refrigerator.

FOR THE KUZU THICKENER

150 g kuzu *(Pueraria lobata)* starch
250 g cold water

Mix the ingredients together and set aside. Stir the preparation every time it is used.

FOR THE PAN-FRIED FERMENTED CABBAGE JUICE

700 g fermented cabbage (previously prepared)
Extra virgin olive oil
60 g kuzu thickener (previously prepared)
Salt

Lightly fry the fermented cabbage in batches with the olive oil in a frying pan and set aside. Transfer to a mixing beaker and lightly chop with a hand-held blender, taking care only to break up the cabbage fibres without turning into a purée.

Put the chopped cabbage into a fine-mesh sieve and use a wooden spoon to press out the juice into a pan. Bring to the boil and add the kuzu thickener in a thin stream while stirring constantly with a whisk until thick. Season with salt if necessary and set aside in a warm place until ready to serve.

FOR THE PARTRIDGE LIVER PARFAIT

200 g partridge livers
200 g unsalted butter
25 g Harveys Bristol Cream sherry
5 g salt
1 g Sichuan pepper

Soak the livers in a container with plenty of water and ice to purge of any blood. Drain and pat dry with kitchen paper.

Cook the livers on both sides in a frying pan with butter, then deglaze the pan with half of the sherry. Transfer to a Thermomix and blend together with the other ingredients and the remaining sherry. Pass the mixture through a fine conical sieve and set aside.

FOR THE GREEN CABBAGE RAVIOLI FILLING

160 g cooked bacon (leftover from preparing the bacon stock)
320 g fermented cabbage (previously prepared)
25 g extra virgin olive oil
50 g The Macallan Fine Oak Triple Cask Matured whisky
120 g bacon stock (previously prepared)
120 g partridge stock (previously prepared)
120 g partridge liver parfait (previously prepared)
2 bay leaves
Pepper
Salt

Finely dice the bacon. Wash the cabbage twice, drain and pat dry with kitchen paper. Brown the bacon in a pan with the olive oil. Add the washed cabbage and sweat until the contents of the pan are soft. Add the whisky and reduce by half. Add the bacon stock, partridge stock, bay leaves and pepper, and cook over a low heat for 1 hour.

Then take out the bay leaves and lightly process with a hand-held blender, taking care not to turn the mixture into a purée. Incorporate the partridge liver parfait. Season with salt and set aside.

PARTRIDGE WITH CABBAGE

FOR THE GREEN CABBAGE RAVIOLI

300 g green cabbage
200 g ravioli filling (previously prepared)
1 kg water
10 g salt
Flour
Extra virgin olive oil

Separate the individual cabbage leaves. Use a 6-cm-diameter round biscuit cutter to cut out discs from the leaves.

Combine the water and salt in a pan and bring to the boil. Blanch the cabbage discs for 1 minute. Refresh quickly in an ice bath, then drain and pat dry with kitchen paper.

Line 2.5-cm-diameter silicone dome moulds with the cabbage discs and fill with the ravioli filling. Close the ravioli by folding over the overhanging edges and pressing. Put a weight over the ravioli and leave for 30 minutes. Turn them out and dust the flat side, where the cabbage leaf has been folded over, with flour. In a frying pan with oil, brown the floured side of the ravioli to seal, to prevent from opening when served. Set aside.

FOR THE CABBAGE AND TARRAGON CREAM

1.36 kg green cabbage
320 g potatoes
160 g unsalted butter
800 g cream
520 g milk
32 g fresh tarragon leaves

Separate the cabbage into individual leaves and use only the whitest leaves for this preparation. Wash and cut the leaves into 5-cm squares and set aside. Peel, wash and dice the potato into a mirepoix.

Melt the butter in a pan over a low heat, then add the cabbage squares and diced potatoes. Turn up the heat and sweat for a few minutes until the cabbage is soft. Add the cream and milk. Cover the pan with a lid and simmer over a low heat for about 20 minutes. Strain the liquid and set aside to cool. Add the tarragon leaves to the cold liquid and blend to a smooth green cream. Strain again and set aside.

FOR THE CABBAGE AND TARRAGON FOAM

800 g cabbage and tarragon cream (previously prepared)
5 g iota carrageenan
3 g salt

Combine the ingredients in a saucepan and bring to the boil. Pour the mixture into a siphon and insert 2 cartridges. Set aside in a bain-marie at 55°C.

FOR THE ROMANESCO

1 head romanesco
1 sprig rosemary
Water
Salt

Wash the romanesco, then use a paring knife to cut into individual florets, preserving the fractal geometry of each. Combine the florets in a bag with a pinch of salt and the rosemary sprig, vacuum seal, and cook in a pan of boiling water for 2 minutes. Cool quickly in an ice bath. Open the bag, remove the cooked florets and set aside.

FOR THE KALE CRISP

100 g kale leaves
Salt
Extra virgin olive oil

Clean the leaves and remove the central rib. Mix the clean leaves with a little salt and oil in a bowl. Spread the leaves out over a tray and put into the oven preheated to 175°C for 10 minutes. The kale should turn crispy without toasting. Season with salt and set aside.

FOR THE KALE JUICE

1 head kale
Salt
Xanthan gum

Separate and wash the kale leaves. Process the leaves in a juicer. Collect the juice and season with salt, then thicken with the xanthan gum. Use 0.2 g of xanthan gum for every 100 g of kale juice. Set aside.

PARTRIDGE WITH CABBAGE

FOR THE CAULIFLOWER FLORETS
1 head cauliflower
500 g water
4 g salt

Wash the cauliflower and separate the florets from the central stalk. Set aside half the florets for the white cauliflower couscous. Blanch the other half in a pan of boiling salted water until tender. Refresh quickly in an ice bath. Then drain and pat dry with kitchen paper. Set aside.

FOR THE WHITE CAULIFLOWER COUSCOUS
½ head cauliflower (set aside from the previous preparation)
1 kg water
8 g salt
Extra virgin olive oil
Black peppercorns

Put the cauliflower inside a Thermomix and grind into small granular pieces. Take care not to grind too finely as this will result in a purée texture. There should be small and loose couscous-like granules.

Bring the water and salt to the boil in a pan. Put the cauliflower couscous into a sieve and immerse in the boiling water to cook. Transfer the sieve to an ice bath to stop the cooking process. Drain off the excess water and pat dry with kitchen paper.

In a bowl, dress the cauliflower with the oil, and season with freshly ground pepper, and salt if necessary. Set aside.

FOR THE RED ARROW BROCCOLI FLORETS
1 head Red Arrow broccoli
500 g water
4 g salt

Combine the water and salt in a pan and bring to the boil. Wash the broccoli, then use a paring knife to cut into 1.5 cm florets. Blanch in the boiling water and quickly refresh in an ice bath. Take the florets out of the water and drain. Pat dry with kitchen paper and set aside.

FOR THE BROCCOLI BUDS
1 head sparaceddu (Sicilian) broccoli
500 g water
3 g salt

Wash the broccoli, then use a paring knife to cut the individual florets from the central stalk and set aside. Combine the water and salt in a pan and bring to the boil. Blanch the broccoli florets for a few seconds in the boiling water and quickly refresh in an ice bath. Drain and pat dry with kitchen paper. Separate the florets into individual buds and set aside.

ASSEMBLY AND FINISHING
Tarragon shoots

Heat the different cabbages (romanesco, cauliflower and broccoli florets, kale crisp, cauliflower couscous and broccoli buds) and the ravioli in the oven at 60°C. Put two tablespoons of pan-fried fermented cabbage juice in the middle of a plate, and make six dots of thickened kale juice around it. Then arrange a green cabbage ravioli, three romanesco florets, a Red Arrow broccoli floret and a white cauliflower floret on the plate. Pipe cabbage and tarragon foam on the plate and flatten into a teardrop with a spoon. Finally, add the partridge breast, which has been rested and kept hot, together with the cauliflower couscous. Finish the dish with a tarragon shoot on the ravioli, a few sparaceddu broccoli buds on the partridge breast, and a kale crisp.

RIB-EYE STEAK

Serves 8

COMPOSITION

—Edible wood
—Candied kumquat
—Black garlic purée
—Caramelised walnuts
—Truffled mayonnaise
—Vanilla oil
—Saffron jelly
—El Ganxet bean *tempeto*
—Rib-eye steak

FOR THE EDIBLE WOOD

1 jar candied wood

Cut the wood into 8-mm squares. Set aside.

FOR THE SIMPLE SUGAR SYRUP

500 g water
500 g sugar

Combine the ingredients in a pan and bring to the boil. Leave to cool and set aside.

FOR THE CANDIED KUMQUAT

100 g kumquats
150 g simple sugar syrup

Combine the kumquats with the syrup in a pan and candy for 2 hours. Drain the kumquats and leave to cool. Cut into 5-mm dice. Set aside.

FOR THE BLACK GARLIC PURÉE

30 cloves black garlic
50 g water
11 g salt
0.75 g xanthan gum (for 100 g purée)

Blend the garlic cloves with the water, salt and xanthan gum. Strain, fill a piping bag and set aside.

FOR THE CARAMELISED WALNUTS

100 g water
60 g sugar
100 g walnuts
40 g icing sugar
Sunflower oil

Combine the water and sugar in a pan and bring to the boil. Add the walnuts and cook over a low heat until they become very tender and almost translucent. Drain and leave to dry on a silicone mat. Use a knife to cut each kernel into quarters and sprinkle with icing sugar. Deep-fry in sunflower oil at 180°C until deep golden and crispy. Take the walnut pieces out of the oil and drain on kitchen paper. Set aside.

FOR THE BLACK TRUFFLE OIL

20 g fresh black truffle, finely diced
100 g extra virgin olive oil

Mix the truffle with the oil and vacuum seal in a bag. Leave to infuse sous-vide in a Roner at 60°C for 2 hours. Remove from the bag and set aside.

FOR THE TRUFFLED MAYONNAISE

25 g egg yolks
10 g water
80 g black truffle oil (previously prepared)
45 g extra virgin olive oil
15 g truffle
Salt

Beat the egg yolk with the water in a bowl until the mixture begins to froth. Gradually add the oils while beating constantly to an emulsion. Finely dice the truffle and add to the mayonnaise. Adjust the seasoning with salt, fill a piping bag and set aside.

FOR THE VANILLA OIL

1 l sunflower oil
5 vanilla pods

Split the vanilla pods and scrape out the seeds with the tip of a knife. Combine the ingredients in a bag and vacuum seal. Cook in a Roner at 65°C for 2 hours. Transfer the infused oil to a squeeze bottle and set aside.

FOR THE SAFFRON JELLY

100 g water
1 g saffron
Salt
1 g agar-agar

Bring the water to the boil in a pan and steep the saffron. Then add the salt and agar-agar and bring back to the boil. Pour into a tray to a depth of 5 mm and leave to cool and set. Cut into 5-mm cubes.

RIB-EYE STEAK

FOR THE EL GANXET BEAN *TEMPETO*

1 kg El Ganxet haricot beans
3 g *Rhizopus Oryzae* fungus spores

Soak the beans for 12 hours to hydrate and to make them easier to peel. Then peel each bean. Boil for 10 minutes, strain and leave to cool.

Sprinkle the beans with the spores and stir to distribute evenly. Put the beans into perforated plastic bags for making tempeh. Leave to ferment at about 30°C for 26 hours, then take the tempeh out of the bags. Vacuum seal in two different bags and cook in a Roner at 55°C. Cook the first bag for 5 days and the second bag for 3 weeks.

Cut both types of *tempeto* into 5-mm cubes. Set aside.

FOR THE BRINE

80 g salt
1 kg water

Combine the water and salt in a pan and bring to the boil. Leave to cool, strain and set aside in a covered container in the refrigerator.

FOR THE RIB-EYE STEAK

1 kg rib-eye steak
Brine (previously prepared)

Immerse the steak in the brine for 25 minutes. Cut the steak into 60-g portions. Finally, sear the steak portions on a barbecue and cut into 6-mm-thick slices.

ASSEMBLY AND FINISHING

Arrange the seared steak in the centre of a plate and the edible wood squares next to it.

Arrange the remaining components of the dish on top of the squares: saffron jelly, caramelised walnut, candied kumquat, truffled mayonnaise, vanilla oil and black garlic purée.

Finish by arranging one 5-day cooked *tempeto* cube and one 3-week cooked *tempeto* cube on the plate.

OAT AND WHISKY COCKTAIL

Serves 8

COMPOSITION
—Oat and whisky cocktail
—Rimmed glass

FOR THE OAT INFUSION
50 g oat malt
300 g still mineral water

Blend the ingredients together. Transfer to a pan and bring to the boil. Strain and set side.

FOR THE OAT AND WHISKY COCKTAIL
1.5 oz The Macallan Rare Cask whisky
1.5 oz oat infusion (previously prepared)
1 oz simple sugar syrup

Mix the three ingredients in a cocktail shaker, shake and serve immediately.

FOR THE COOKED OATS
50 g rolled oats
500 g water
2 g salt

Soak the oats in 250 g of water in a container for at least 12 hours in the refrigerator. Then drain and combine the oats with the remaining water in a pan. Bring to the boil and cook for about 20 minutes. Take out the cooked oats, drain off the excess water and dry. Set aside.

FOR THE SUGAR-COATED OATS
50 g cooked oats (previously prepared)
25 g sugar
15 g water
Salt

Spread the cooked oats over a silicone mat, spacing apart. Dry out in a dehydrator at 55°C for about 1 hour 30 minutes. Remove and set aside.

Mix the water with the sugar in a pan and bring to the boil. Then add the oats and leave over the heat without allowing the oats to colour. As the water evaporates, the sugar will begin to crystallise. Then remove the pan from the heat and allow the water to continue to evaporate until all the oats develop a sugar coating. Season with salt. In a mortar, lightly crush the sugar-coated oats without grinding to a powder. Set aside.

FOR THE RIMMED GLASS
20 g pasteurised egg white
50 g sugar-coated oats (previously prepared)

To rim the glass, put the egg white in a container and the lightly crushed sugar-coated oats in another. Hold the cocktail glass upside down and lightly dip the rim in the egg white. Then dip in the sugar-coated oats, which will stick to the rim. Set aside until ready to serve.

ASSEMBLY AND FINISHING
Crushed ice
Almond flowers

Chill the glass with crushed ice. Pour in the well-shaken cocktail. Serve with almond flowers.

ABERDEEN ANGUS BEEF SHOULDER WITH MORELS, CELERIAC AND TARRAGON

Serves 8

COMPOSITION

—Aberdeen Angus beef shoulder
—Aberdeen Angus beef sauce
—Aberdeen Angus beef marrow
—Aberdeen Angus beef tendon
—Celeriac and tarragon purée
—Black olive earth
—Morel purée
—Sautéed morels

FOR THE BRINE

3 kg water
300 g salt

Completely dissolve the salt in the water in a container. Cover with a lid and refrigerate.

FOR THE ABERDEEN ANGUS BEEF SHOULDER

1 kg Aberdeen Angus beef chuck and blade (shoulder)
2 l brine (previously prepared)
Extra virgin olive oil

Put the meat into a container, cover with brine and soak for 2 hours. Then take it out and dry well.

Heat a little oil in a frying pan and sear the meat on all sides. Next, cool quickly, vacuum seal in a bag and cook in the oven at 55°C for 72 hours. Cool quickly and refrigerate.

FOR THE ABERDEEN ANGUS BEEF SAUCE

350 g Aberdeen Angus beef trimmings
350 g Aberdeen Angus beef bones
70 g onions
50 g leeks
40 g celery
35 g carrot
35 g extra virgin olive oil
10 g unsalted butter
150 g red wine
650 g water
40 g Manzanilla sherry
0.3 g black peppercorns

Put the beef bones on a tray and roast in the oven at 180°C for 45 minutes. Dice the vegetables into a mirepoix.

Heat the oil and butter in a pan and add the vegetables. Then add the meat and brown for a few minutes. Add the roasted bones. Incorporate the wine and reduce until all the alcohol has evaporated. Add the water and peppercorns and cook over a medium heat for 1 hour. Next, add the sherry and reduce for 20 more minutes. Strain the mixture and leave to cool. Use a spoon to remove the fat from the surface. Transfer the sauce to a pan and reduce by half over a medium heat. Set aside.

FOR THE ABERDEEN ANGUS BEEF MARROW

250 g Aberdeen Angus beef marrow
Salt
Pepper
Flour
Extra virgin olive oil

Put the marrow into a container filled with water and ice, cover and soak in the refrigerator for 24 hours to purge of any blood. Change the water every 6 hours, adding more ice if necessary. Then take out the marrow, pat dry with kitchen paper and cut into 1-cm-thick slices. Immediately before serving, season with salt and pepper, dredge in flour and sear on a griddle with a little oil.

FOR THE ABERDEEN ANGUS BEEF TENDON

100 g Aberdeen Angus beef tendons
250 g brine (previously prepared)
Soy sauce

Put the tendons into a container with the brine and soak for 30 minutes. Transfer to a pan with cold water and bring to the boil to blanch. Take out the tendons, discard the water and refill with cold water, and cook the tendons for 3 hours over a medium heat at a low boil. Transfer the tendons to a tray, setting aside the cooking liquid, and cool quickly. When cold, clean and cut into 1-cm-thick slices. Set aside in a bain-marie covered in their cooking water with an added tablespoon of soy sauce.

FOR THE CELERIAC AND TARRAGON PURÉE

500 g celeriac
100 g leeks, white only
10 g extra virgin olive oil
1.5 kg water
10 g tarragon
40 g unsalted butter

Pluck the tarragon leaves and weigh out 10 g.

Clean the leeks and cut into 2-cm-thick slices. Peel, wash and cut the celeriac into large chunks. In a pan with the oil, brown the leek slices on both sides. Add the water and celeriac and bring to the boil. Cook for about 15 minutes and strain. Pick out the celeriac pieces and blend with the tarragon and butter in a Thermomix. Set aside and keep warm.

FOR THE BLACK OLIVE EARTH

400 g black olive paste
500 g flour
50 g Royal baking powder
325 g unsalted butter, softened
50 g glucose
24 g icing sugar
10 eggs
Salt

Sift the flour and mix with the baking powder.

Cream the butter with the icing sugar and glucose in a mixer. When fluffy, whisk in the eggs one at a time. Add the flour and baking powder mixture. Finally, fold in the olive paste and season with salt if necessary.

Grease a baking pan and fill with the batter. Bake in the oven for about 6 minutes at 165°C, then raise the temperature to 180°C and bake for 8 more minutes. Use a toothpick to check that the cake is cooked. Take out of the oven and rest on a rack. Crumble to make the black olive earth. Set aside.

ABERDEEN ANGUS BEEF SHOULDER WITH MORELS, CELERIAC AND TARRAGON

FOR THE MOREL PURÉE
600 g fresh morels
80 g shallots
40 g unsalted butter
270 g cream
6 g salt

Wash the morels in cold water. Cut off and discard the stem and cut each mushroom in half.

Finely dice the shallot and sauté with the butter in a frying pan until golden. Add the morels and continue to sauté for a few minutes. Add the salt and cream and continue to cook until it begins to boil. Strain and set aside the morels and cooking liquid separately.

300 g cooked morels
150 g morel cooking liquid
Salt

Mix the morels with the cooking liquid and blend with a hand-held blender. Press through a drum sieve, season with salt and set aside.

FOR THE ROSEMARY AND GARLIC OIL
200 g extra virgin olive oil
45 g fresh morels
5 g garlic
2 sprigs rosemary
2 g salt

Peel and crush the garlic cloves. Cut the morels into large pieces.

Combine all the ingredients in a pan and heat to 80°C. Take the pan off the heat and leave to infuse for 1 hour. Then strain, leave to cool and set aside.

FOR THE SAUTÉED MORELS
16 small morels
Rosemary and garlic oil (previously prepared)
Salt

Clean and wash the morels well. Sauté in a frying pan with the oil. Season with salt and set aside.

ASSEMBLY AND FINISHING
Tender turnip leaves
Sherry vinegar
Extra virgin olive oil
Salt flakes

Open the vacuum bag and remove the cooked beef shoulder. Cut into 80-g rectangular portions. Vacuum seal each portion inside a bag with two tablespoons of sauce per portion. Immediately before serving, reheat to 55°C for at least 15 minutes.

Spread a teardrop of morel purée and another of celeriac and tarragon purée on a flat plate. Arrange a freshly seared marrow slice on one side of the plate and top with a tendon slice. Dress the turnip leaves with vinegar and oil and season with salt. Put a turnip leaf over the celeriac and tarragon purée and add a pinch of black olive earth beside it. Finish by arranging a piece of Aberdeen Angus beef shoulder covered with sauce and two freshly sautéed morels.

WHISKY TARTLET

Makes 25

COMPOSITION
—Shortcrust pastry
—Whisky ganache

FOR THE SHORTCRUST PASTRY
1 kg plain flour
500 g sugar
400 g unsalted butter
300 g eggs
50 g cocoa powder
7 g baking powder

Sift the flour with the cocoa and baking powder into a bowl. In another bowl, cream the butter with the sugar until fluffy. Whisk in the eggs one at a time. When fully incorporated, transfer to a mixer and add the powders a third at a time while mixing on low speed using the flat beater attachment. Cover the pastry with cling film in contact with the surface and set aside in the refrigerator.

FOR THE WHISKY GANACHE
475 g dark couverture chocolate (64% cocoa)
350 g cream
75 g unsalted butter
75 g invert sugar
35 g The Macallan Double Cask 12 Years Old whisky

Combine the couverture with the butter in a Thermomix. Combine the cream with the invert sugar in a pan and bring to the boil. Then add the mixture to the Thermomix. Beat on medium speed until very smooth. Incorporate the whisky and set aside.

ASSEMBLY AND FINISHING
Pasteurised egg yolk
Edible silver leaf

Use a rolling pin to roll out the pastry to a 1-mm thickness. Line tartlet moulds with the pastry and rest for at least 30 minutes.

Bake the tartlet shells at 180°C for 5 minutes with 0% humidity and a medium fan. Take the shells out of the oven and brush with a fine layer of egg yolk. Return to the oven and bake for 1 more minute.

Leave to cool a little, then turn the shells out of the moulds while still warm. Fill with the ganache and leave to set. Decorate the tartlets with silver leaf.

BRIOCHE FILLED WITH WHISKY-BRAISED LAMB'S KIDNEYS

Serves 8

COMPOSITION
—Brioche
—Whisky-braised lamb's kidneys

FOR THE BRIOCHE
36 g sugar
30 g milk
14.4 g yeast
150 g eggs
300 g flour
150 g softened butter
3.6 g salt

Add the sugar and yeast to the milk in a bowl and mix until fully dissolved. Add the eggs. Sift the flour twice and incorporate one half at a time into the mixture. Add the butter and salt. Knead the dough until it is smooth and elastic, and it comes away from the sides of the bowl. Transfer to another bowl, cover and rest in the refrigerator for 12 hours.

Use a rolling pin and a little flour to roll out the dough between two sheets of baking parchment. Rest in the refrigerator for 30 minutes, then cut into 6-g portions and return to the refrigerator. Shape the individual dough portions into balls and proof for 40 minutes at 40°C with 45% humidity.

Pre-heat the oven to 135°C without humidity and set the vent to position 4. Bake the brioche buns for 4–5 minutes. They should be cooked through but must not change colour.

CLEANING THE KIDNEYS
250 g lamb's kidneys
Water
Ice

Remove any fat and membranes from the kidneys. Put them in a large bowl with ice and water and purge for 12 hours. Keep the bowl in the refrigerator, changing the water every 3 hours and adding more ice if necessary. Then take out the kidneys, drain off the excess water and pat dry with kitchen paper. Set aside.

FOR THE WHISKY-BRAISED LAMB'S KIDNEYS
250 g cleaned lamb's kidneys (previously prepared)
4 g parsley
3 cloves garlic
50 g The Macallan Double Cask 12 Years Old whisky
3.5 g salt
Extra virgin olive oil

Wash the parsley, pat dry with kitchen paper and finely chop. Peel and remove the green core from the garlic cloves, then finely dice.

Cut the kidneys into 3-mm-thin slices. In a frying pan over a low heat, sauté the garlic in a little olive oil without colouring. When the garlic is well sweated and soft, raise the heat and add the kidney slices. Sauté, then add the whisky. Reduce the cooking liquid and season with salt. Add the chopped parsley when the kidneys are cooked. Mix, then take out the kidneys and set aside separately from the sauce.

ASSEMBLY AND FINISHING
Fresh thyme leaves

But the brioche buns inside a bamboo steamer basket and steam to reheat. Once soft and hot, use a serrated knife to cut each bun in half across the middle. Lightly spread the cut side of the bun halves with the sauce. Fill with the whisky-braised kidney slices, garlic and parsley, and add 3–4 fresh thyme leaves. Serve hot.

LOIN OF VENISON WITH PEPPERS

Serves 8

COMPOSITION

—Venison loin
—The Macallan Rare Cask Black venison sauce
—White pepper jelly
—Pink pepper jelly
—Allspice jelly
—Black pepper jelly

FOR THE BRINE

2 kg water
200 g salt

Completely dissolve the salt in the cold water in a container. Cover with a lid and refrigerate.

FOR THE VENISON LOIN

2 venison loins
2 kg brine (previously prepared)
Extra virgin olive oil

Clean the loins, put into a container and cover with the brine. Leave to rest for 2 hours. Then drain and pat dry with kitchen paper.

Heat a little extra virgin oil in a frying pan and sear the meat on all sides. Rest the meat for about 8 minutes.

FOR THE VENISON JUS

350 g venison trimmings
1 kg venison bones
50 g leek
70 g onion
40 g celery
35 g carrot
150 g red wine
35 g extra virgin olive oil
10 g unsalted butter
1.35 kg water
0.3 g black peppercorns
Salt

Dice the vegetables into a mirepoix, put into a pan with the oil and brown well over a low heat.

Put the bones and trimmings into a roasting tin and roast in the oven at 200°C until golden. Remove the excess fat and transfer to a stock pot together with the mirepoix. Deglaze the caramelised juices in the roasting tin with water and add the liquid to the pot. Cover the contents of the pot with cold water and the red wine, and cook over a low heat for about 2 hours.

Then strain and reduce the liquid to 200 g. Season with salt and thicken with the butter. Set aside.

FOR THE KUZU THICKENER

150 g kuzu *(Pueraria lobata)* starch
250 g cold water

Mix the ingredients together and set aside. Stir the preparation every time it is used.

FOR THE MACALLAN RARE CASK BLACK VENISON SAUCE

200 g venison jus (previously prepared)
Kuzu thickener (previously prepared)
20 g The Macallan Rare Cask Black whisky
10 g unsalted butter
Salt

Bring the venison jus to a boil in a pan and add the kuzu thickener, stirring briskly with a whisk to the desired consistency. Finally, incorporate the whisky, mix well and whisk in the butter. Season with salt and set aside.

FOR THE WHITE PEPPER INFUSION
100 g still mineral water
1.2 g white peppercorns

Use a spice mill to grind the peppercorns immediately before use. Combine the water and the freshly ground white pepper in a container and leave to steep in the refrigerator for 30 minutes. Strain the infusion through a fine-mesh sieve lined with kitchen paper. Set aside.

FOR THE WHITE PEPPER JELLY
100 g white pepper infusion (previously prepared)
1 g agar-agar
Freshly ground white pepper

Sprinkle a pinch of pepper over the bottom of 5 x 2.5-cm and 1-cm-high rectangular moulds.

Mix the white pepper infusion with the agar-agar in a saucepan and bring to the boil, then fill the prepared moulds. Leave to set in the refrigerator.

Unmould the jelly and cut into 2.5 x 1-cm and 1-cm-thick rectangles. Set aside.

FOR THE PINK PEPPER INFUSION
100 g still mineral water
1.2 g pink peppercorns

Grind the peppercorns in a mortar immediately before use. Combine the water and the freshly ground pink pepper in a container and leave to steep in the refrigerator for 30 minutes. Strain the infusion through a fine-mesh sieve lined with kitchen paper. Set aside.

FOR THE PINK PEPPER JELLY
100 g pink pepper infusion (previously prepared)
1 g agar-agar
Freshly ground pink pepper

Sprinkle a pinch of pepper over the bottom of 5 x 2.5-cm and 1-cm-high rectangular moulds.

Mix the pink pepper infusion with the agar-agar in a saucepan and bring to the boil, then fill the prepared moulds. Leave to set in the refrigerator.

Unmould the jelly and cut into 2.5 x 1-cm and 1-cm-thick rectangles. Set aside.

FOR THE ALLSPICE INFUSION
100 g still mineral water
1.2 g allspice berries

Use a spice mill to grind the allspice berries immediately before use. Combine the water and the freshly ground allspice in a container and leave to steep in the refrigerator for 30 minutes. Strain the infusion through a fine-mesh sieve lined with kitchen paper. Set aside.

FOR THE ALLSPICE JELLY
100 g allspice infusion (previously prepared)
1 g agar-agar
Freshly ground allspice

Sprinkle a pinch of allspice over the bottom of 5 x 2.5-cm and 1-cm-high rectangular moulds.

Mix the allspice infusion with the agar-agar in a saucepan and bring to the boil, then fill the prepared moulds. Leave to set in the refrigerator.

Unmould the jelly and cut into 2.5 x 1-cm and 1-cm-thick rectangles. Set aside.

LOIN OF VENISON WITH PEPPERS

FOR THE BLACK PEPPER INFUSION
100 g still mineral water
1.2 g black peppercorns

Use a spice mill to grind the peppercorns immediately before use. Combine the water and the freshly ground black pepper in a container and leave to steep in the refrigerator for 30 minutes. Strain the infusion through a fine-mesh sieve lined with kitchen paper. Set aside.

FOR THE BLACK PEPPER JELLY
100 g black pepper infusion (previously prepared)
1 g agar-agar
Freshly ground black pepper

Sprinkle a pinch of pepper over the bottom of 5 x 2.5-cm and 1-cm-high rectangular moulds.

Mix the black pepper infusion with the agar-agar in a saucepan and bring to the boil, then fill the prepared moulds. Leave to set in the refrigerator.

Unmould the jelly and cut into 2.5 x 1-cm and 1-cm-thick rectangles. Set aside.

ASSEMBLY AND FINISHING
Freshly ground white pepper
Freshly ground pink pepper
Freshly ground allspice
Freshly ground black pepper

Immediately before serving, carve five slices of the rested venison loin per person. Lightly heat under a salamander grill.

In the centre of a plate, make four dots of the venison sauce and lay a slice of venison loin over each one.

Heat the jelly rectangles and place in the following order on top of the venison slices: white pepper, pink pepper, allspice and black pepper, accompanied by a pinch of each spice on one side of the meat.

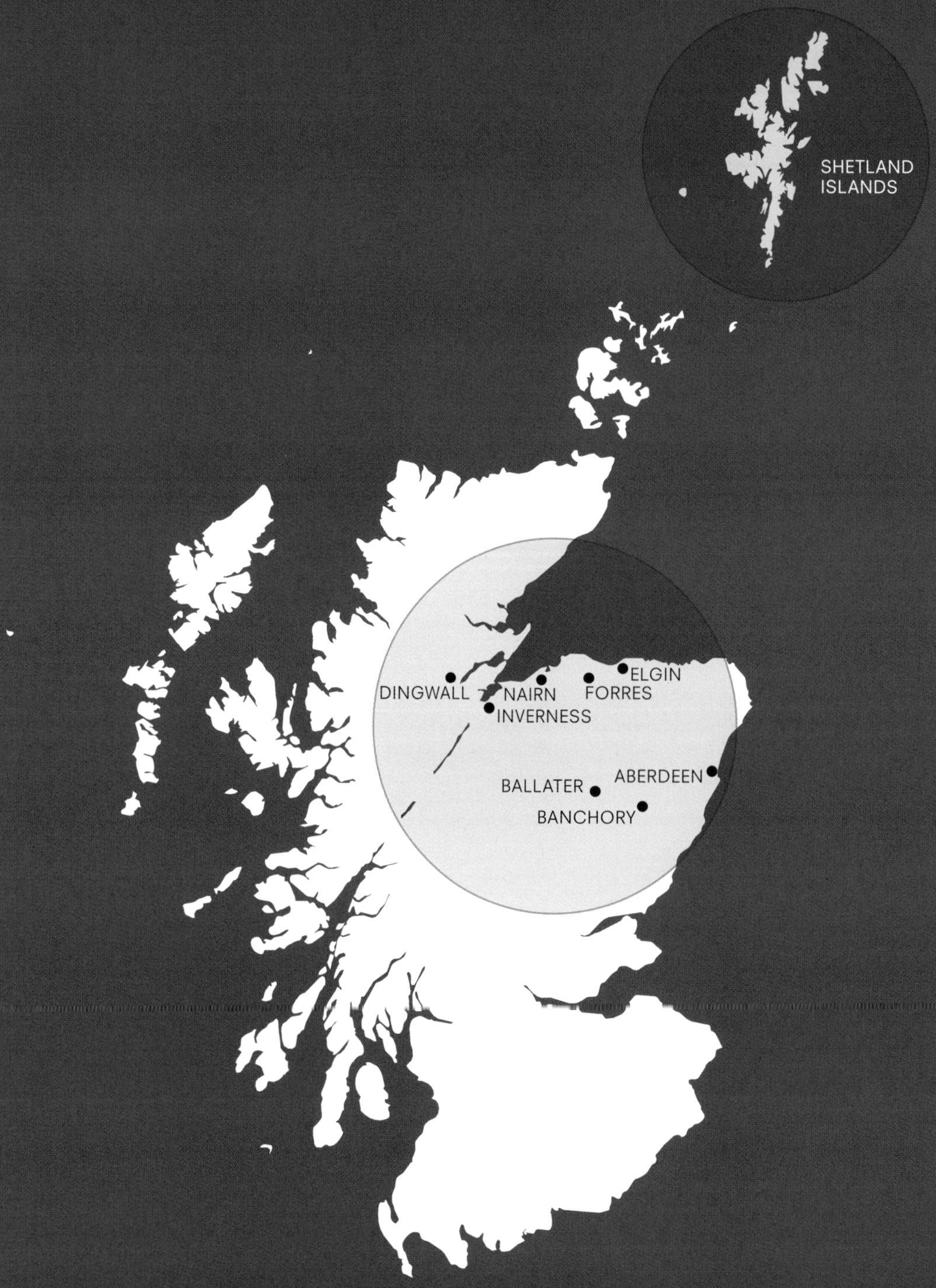
SHETLAND
ISLANDS
ELGIN
DINGWALL
NAIRN
FORRES
INVERNESS
ABERDEEN
BALLATER
BANCHORY

NORTH COAST AND THE SHETLAND ISLANDS

'We came in the afternoon to Slanes[1] Castle, built upon the margin of the sea, so that the walls of one of the towers seem only a continuation of a perpendicular rock, the foot of which is beaten by the waves [...] I would not for my amusement wish for a storm; but as storms, whether wished or not, will sometimes happen, I may say, without violation of humanity, that I should willingly look out upon them from Slanes Castle.'[2] Johnson's description of the castle, set against the backdrop of Cruden bay, paints a striking picture. It remains so today, and, if possible, is even more dramatic, as it is now in ruins and has lost its roof. It is as if the power of the sea and wind has succeeded in converting the walls into breakwaters. The jagged cliffs surrounding the castle are marked with cracks, crevices and arches — all that remain of collapsed caverns — and reinforce the image of a merciless sea.

Slains Castle could be Count Dracula's Castle. On seeing this skeleton of stones amongst the crags, anyone who has read Bram Stoker's novel could imagine that this is the residence of the Un-Dead[3]. They would be on the right track: Stoker visited the area from 1880 and nearby locations actually appear in some of his other works. It is not unreasonable, therefore, to hazard a guess that this mansion built by the Earl of Errol, which a century earlier caught Johnson's eye with its exposure to nature's sheer power, could have partly inspired the Irish author's Transylvania castle in his late-nineteenth-century romantic novel. In this case, as in many others, fiction feeds from reality to create a more credible image.

---

1 Nowadays it is spelled Slains.

2 Johnson, S. (1984, p. 45). *A Journey to the Western Islands of Scotland*. London: Penguin Classics.

3 The Un-Dead was the title Stoker was going to use to publish the novel until he changed it at the last minute to Dracula.

Previous page: Coastal landscape of the Shetland Islands

However, sometimes the opposite is true: reality loses its credibility because of the mistakes made by the person relaying it. While Johnson and Boswell were staying in the house of Mr Ferne, the warehouse manager at Fort George, James Boswell leafed through Thomas Pennant's book *A Tour of Scotland in 1769*, reading his description of the fort at which they had just arrived. However, what Boswell saw *in situ* didn't match with the Welsh writer's description. The mismatch between the narration and reality was enough for the two writers and their host to discuss the topic. Johnson, for whom Pennant's book, which was published a couple of years previously, was one of the finest examples of a travel journal, ends up acknowledging that people's descriptions don't often match up with reality. According to Johnson, the reason was, 'that people do not write them till some time after, and then their imagination has added circumstances'.[4] Johnson published his book about his travels in Scotland two years after setting out on the journey and Boswell, who recorded the doctor's phrase, published his some thirteen years later.

In non-fiction, the intention of documenting and relaying reality can come up against bias in the author's perspective or a lack of skill. Therefore, involuntarily, the writer doesn't communicate the required information. In this case, the innocent reader only realises the error when, just like the two travellers, they have the opportunity to verify what they read. In fiction, however, the writer and reader are both accomplices to the deception and this is an unspoken agreement that allows the story to come alive. Bram Stoker uses scientific reasoning, blood transfusions and Cartesian characters to tell this unlikely, romantic myth of the vampire. They are the pieces of bait that are left out to build this deceit and win over the reader.

---

4 Boswell, J. (1807, p.112). *The Journal of a Tour to the Hebrides.* London: T. Cadwell and W. Davies.

Josep, River Dee, near Ballater

Bait, tricks, decoys and camouflage: hunting and fishing are also a kind of deceit, a fiction that is created with the aim of catching the prey. The only defence the animal has is its intuition, smell and perhaps a genetic warning system from generations of being hunted by mankind. There seems to be nothing noble about this uneven fight, but in fact, out of the sense of superiority in the confrontation, comes a feeling of submission to nature.

There is something mystical about fishing salmon in a Scottish river, even if you achieve only minor success. The natural environment, the silence which is hardly broken by the burbling of the river or the chirps of birds, the solitude... all of these factors that accompany fishing serve to encourage contemplation. Keeping your balance while stood on the riverbed, with water up to your hips and small whirlpools passing by your rubber boots, certainly makes you think about life.

Fishing, just like hunting, is an exercise in modesty and arrogance at the same time. It is probably this duality that makes these activities somewhat controversial. The insignificance of humanity becomes more evident in the midst of nature. This is even more apparent when you have a fishing rod in your hands, in an exercise of patience that isn't always successful. In this case, even when you do catch a fish, all it provides, after many failures, is a feeling of victory over the salmon's cunning, because there's no material reward: by law, the salmon must be returned to the water to guarantee the survival of the species.

Josep on the Shetland Islands

Fishing and salmon are still essential in gaining an understanding of Scottish cuisine. With this aim in mind, Josep meets Martin Robson on the banks of the River Dee, near Ballater. The Dee meets the sea some 40 kilometres south of Slains Castle, in Aberdeen. Just like many Scottish rivers, it is a salmon river. However, for years, the sale and consumption of fished salmon has been banned. From its source in the Cairngorms National Park, the Dee flows 140 kilometres west, with half of its length running through the park. Balmoral Castle, the Royal Family's Scottish residence, can be found on one of its meanders.

Martin is a self-taught fisherman who, from February to October, during the salmon fishing season, devotes five days a week to his passion. Martin explains the salmon-fishing techniques to Josep, how you should cast the line, keep it tense and guide the bait so that it floats along the correct route down river, parallel to the bank. This ritual is illustrated with gestures and quietly spoken words, as it is essential to not raise the suspicions of the Atlantic salmon, common trout and brown trout which are the most commonly found species in the River Dee. While they wait – fishing is an activity that requires patience – Josep talks to Martin about the salmon's head, which is disproportionately small compared to its body. He wants to know if Martin likes to eat the cheeks, *cocochas*,[5] nose and belly... the fisherman replies that the idea interests him, but that he has never tried them. It must be a question of cultural difference: it's not common to find whole fish in restaurants or fishmongers; usually they just sell cleaned and deboned fillets.

---

5 The gelatinous part found in the throat of certain large fish, eaten in Spain.

In December 2015, this seemingly tranquil river burst its banks during Storm Frank and swept away everything in its path. Ballater was one of the worst affected areas. Thanks to some support and the high level of interest in restoring the region's economy, the restaurant Rothesay[6] Rooms was founded, amongst other projects. The generosity of individuals and local groups was added to by crucial backing from Prince Charles's foundation and it opened in 2016. One year later, it received its first Michelin star.

Here, the need to support the area's economy, which has been key since the project's beginnings, makes using local products a moral obligation. The restaurant chef, Ross Cochrane, is a committed advocate of this approach, 'Amongst chefs, the idea has grown that, just as we don't use certain products because of their rarity, we should use local products that need to be promoted, instead of exporting them to France or sending them to London, for example'. As Ross himself says, they are lucky to be in this area because the local products are incredible: lamb, deer, geese, grouse, fish, etc. He's talking about the location of Rothesay Rooms, but his statement could apply to the whole of the country. As he says, 'Here we're surrounded by products that we consider to be the pride of the nation, there is a huge amount of exceptionally high-quality raw materials available.'

---

6 The dynastic title of Prince Charles.

'THERE IS SOMETHING MYSTICAL ABOUT FISHING SALMON IN A SCOTTISH RIVER. ALL THE FACTORS THAT ACCOMPANY FISHING SERVE TO ENCOURAGE CONTEMPLATION. KEEPING YOUR BALANCE WHILE STOOD ON THE RIVERBED, WITH WATER UP TO YOUR HIPS AND SMALL WHIRLPOOLS PASSING BY YOUR RUBBER BOOTS, CERTAINLY MAKES YOU THINK ABOUT LIFE.'

—JOSEP ROCA

Martin Robson, ghillie of Little Blackhall & Inchmarlo Fishings, fishing in the River Dee

SCOTLAND: A COUNTRY FOR HUNTERS

On the outskirts of Trochry, Josep meets James, Mark and Jake, part of the management board of the British Association for Shooting & Conservation Scotland (BASC), which was founded 50 years ago with the aim of regulating this hobby. The following of certain rules – by hunters and hunting ground owners alike – has contributed to the conservation of bird species whose populations had been decimated for years by uncontrolled hunting. Fortunately, the area is still a reserve for many of these birds: geese arrive from Greenland and Iceland, and ducks from Russia and Finland. These birds migrate when they start to feel the cold and make their journey to warmer climes. Some of them stay in Scotland; for others it's just a stopover on their way south.

Scotland is a country for hunters. At times when there is very scarce game at other latitudes, such as in Spain, either because of a lack of water or the exhaustion of resources due to construction or intensive agriculture, this resource becomes an excellent source of income. There is not only an abundance of birds: indeed, the overpopulation of deer in Scotland is a high-priority political problem and up until now plans that have been implemented to reduce their numbers have not worked. With a total of 750,000 deer, steps have included killing 100,000 animals a year and substantial fines for any landowners who do not comply with the quotas.

This huge number of deer is the result of an imbalance that, while aggravated over the last 50 years, has existed for centuries, probably since landowners forced sharecroppers to leave their land so that it could be used for intensive livestock farming and logging. The chopping down of native forests to prepare the land for breeding deer only worsened the problem. The immediate consequences were deforestation, which Johnson was already reporting in the late eighteenth century. The gradual disappearance of the forests led to a drop in the number of predators and their absence caused an uncontrolled increase in deer numbers. This explosion of the deer population made reforestation impossible, because one of deer's favourite foods is young tree seedlings. Therefore, it has become unfeasible to recuperate the forest cover.

You can often find venison dishes on restaurant menus and in processed meats: sausages, hamburgers, pies, etc. Despite this fact, most of the deer that are killed are exported and the parts received by the hunters that cannot be sold, are for individual consumption. The practice of hunting, which has now become a hobby, connects us with a past of brave men whose survival depended on their ability to hunt. Today, with the use of firearms, the two sides are unbalanced, but it still retains some of its mystical charm.

Jake Swindells and Mark Astley Jones of the BASC

I confess my prior reservations about hunting and hunters to James, Mark and Jake. These were no doubt a result of my lack of knowledge about this hobby. It had always seemed like a cruel and inhumane activity to me; perhaps because I had never stopped to think that, accepting the premise that meat is part of our diet, being shot at close range is a dignified death for a wild animal. Even more so when compared with the practice of intensive farming, in which the well-being of the animal is often ignored.

Aside from these considerations, what has probably most shaped my opinion about hunting is talking to the three men and realising that a passion for hunting and love of nature often come hand in hand. As the writer Miguel Delibes said, 'I love nature because I'm a hunter. I'm a hunter because I love nature.' In this phrase he brings together two destinies that seem to be contradictory, but that are actually found united in almost everyone who goes hunting or fishing. What is more, neither of these activities can be completely understood without the promise of a delicious feast at the end. This perspective is shared by the hunters as well as by me. In fact, it is in their company that I remember having the best culinary experience.

‘A forest and in the forest: the deer. [...] King Lear — an old king who ruled the Celtic sea — ate deer every day to prepare his spirit for justice: it was roasted in front of his tent, was soaked in rye and apple liquor and sheep lard, and served by the nobles to the king in large pieces on the tip of the sword Calibarte.’[7] There’s no doubt that culinary pleasure is one of the reasons behind hunting today. But it has always been present, as revealed by the number of recipe books about hunting as well as the books that culinary writers, such as Álvaro Cunqueiro, have written on the topic. And of course there are countless still-life paintings that, for centuries, have depicted game about to be prepared for an exquisite feast.

Josep also talks to the hunters about cuisine; he wants to find out whether they leave the meat to mature and asks them about their family recipes. ‘When it’s cold, we leave it to mature. The process of hanging it (*faisandage* in French) allows the flavours to develop and makes the meat more tender,’ says James. In his house, they usually eat whole, roasted birds. Jake also tells Josep about how he uses the whole of the deer that he’s shot. With game, making the most of everything isn’t just an economic consideration, it is ethical: having killed a wild animal the hunter is obliged to make use of the whole of the animal. It is as if this were the only way to justify the death. One of the examples he gives is the deer heart, which he prepares by smoking it. Even when hunters could sell the deer they shot, eating the heart was a privilege reserved for the person who killed it. The right to eat the heart of the victim, the organ containing its driving force, energy and soul, is one the most symbolic aspects of hunting and, for many, the most primeval and captivating part.

---

7 Castroviejo, J.M. y Cunqueiro, Á. (4th Edition, 1986). *Viaje por los Montes y Chimeneas de Galicia. Caza y Cocina Gallegas.* Madrid: Espasa Calpe.

‘Scottish game is the very best; restaurants around the world buy our grouse.’ This is David Littlewood, the owner of Tor-Na-Coille Hotel in Banchory and president of the Federation of Chefs of Scotland, who speaks with such pride. Regarding the changes that have happened in Scottish cuisine over recent years, he says, ‘We live in a cold country and our traditional cuisine is heavy, but the world has become smaller, everything is more accessible and today we’re looking towards the Mediterranean, Asia and Scandinavia. We take influences from around the world. People are travelling and keen to learn more about cooking.’

Rothesay Rooms restaurant

THE BREAKFASTS OF KINGS

This third trip is one in which Josep's route leaves the path taken by the two eighteenth-century authors. The main reason is that Johnson and Boswell only ventured inland to cross from Inverness to Glenelg where they took the boat to the Isle of Skye. However, products like game, which are a key part of Scottish cuisine, are found further inland. For this reason, Josep doesn't hesitate to leave the writers' route to get to know these products first-hand.

Johnson and Boswell continued north along the coast first and then headed west to arrive at Inverness. In Elgin they wrote about the first bad food that they had come across on the trip. Samuel Johnson wrote, 'About noon [we] came to Elgin, where in the inn [...] a dinner was set before us, which we could not eat.'[8] It wasn't a usual occurrence, although they came across many houses and inns where, either because they weren't used to eating certain products, certain raw materials were scarce or the table manners left something to be desired, the travellers weren't completely satisfied. On the other hand, they were full of praise for Scottish breakfasts. 'If our dinners and suppers remain more distinctive than distinguished, we can reflect with satisfaction that our breakfasts and teas, at their best, are nowhere surpassed.'[9] This quote comes from a 1929 cookery book, but the Englishman Johnson had already highlighted the importance of this first meal of the day that the Scots like to praise, 'If an epicure could remove by a wish, in quest of sensual gratifications, wherever he had supped he would breakfast in Scotland.' [10]

---

8 Johnson, S. (1984, p. 48). *A Journey to the Western Islands of Scotland*. London: Penguin Classics.

9 McNeill, F. M. (1929). *The Scots Kitchen: Its Traditions and Lore with Old-Time Recipes*. Glasgow: Blackie & Son Limited.

10 Johnson, S. (1984, p. 48). *A Journey to the Western Islands of Scotland*. London: Penguin Classics.

MACBETH AND MACBETH

With Johnson and Boswell continuing their route westwards from Elgin and Josep heading towards the north coast to visit some farms, their paths cross again near Forres, in the middle of a barren plain, surrounded by wisps of fog. It is a literary meeting, also attended by Macbeth and Banquo, who asks, 'How far is't call'd to Forres? What are these So wither'd and so wild in their attire, That look not like the inhabitants o' the earth, And yet are on't? Live you?'[11] Appearing from the mist, their hands clasped together, three spirits can be seen:

'All hail, Macbeth! hail to thee, thane of Glamis!
All hail, Macbeth, hail to thee, thane of Cawdor!
All hail, Macbeth, thou shalt be king hereafter!'

And after making this prophecy about Macbeth, they fade away through the heather.

Some locations have a special magnetism, like this sparse, inhospitable plain on which William Shakespeare set this scene of his 1606 play. In this case, the description of the place and what can be seen today, 400 years later, match each other well: reality flirts again with fiction.

---

11 Shakespeare, W. (2008). *The Oxford Shakespeare: The Tragedy of Macbeth*. Oxford: Oxford University Press. This same scene (Act I, Scene III) is mentioned by James Boswell in his book. On this part of the journey, Johnson also alludes to the three witches that made the prophecy to Macbeth. The play locates Duncan's Castle, that Banquo asks about here, in Forres.

The farm that Josep visits in Forres is called Edinvale Farm. Jock Gibson, whose parents bought the farm in the mid-1970s, meets him. 'I want my children and grandchildren to be able to continue living from this, I don't want to use up all the resources,' he says, thinking of the generation that will take over from him. In response to Josep's questions, Jock admits that intensive farming has a serious impact on the environment, but that there are ways to minimise the damage, 'We use specific measures, voluntarily, to reduce our carbon emissions'. According to Jock, in Scotland, most production is carried out in wide areas, using extensive livestock farming, like on Edinvale Farm. Even so, there is still room for improvement, 'Now, we're thinking about how to store the hay in a way that doesn't create so much waste and saves energy at the same time. My wife, Fiona, is also starting to breed lambs. This will not only diversify our business, but also gives us more control as we'll be farming them ourselves. If we control it then we can also improve it,' says Jock.

On Edinvale Farm, they cross three local cattle breeds: Highland, Aberdeen Angus and Shorthorn. 'My father started this business with two Highland cows. The meat from Highland cattle tastes great, although they don't produce as much as other breeds,' explains Gibson. It takes two and a half years for the meat to be ready for sale and all this time is completely wasted if a mistake is made at slaughter or in the distribution process.

Despite the deep-rooted livestock farming culture and the high value of beef, not everything is made use of from the carcass. ‘In the United Kingdom, the most valued parts are the loin and hindquarter cuts, there are many other parts that are used in the rest of Europe, but which here are made into minced meat for processed products,’ says Jock, who mentions the 17 cuts that are used, compared to 84 that he has discovered you can buy in France. By way of an example, he says, ‘I have a client, a restaurant, that uses the cheeks, but it’s not that common.’ ‘In my opinion the best part is the rump, although many of the cuts found around the shoulder blade, like feather blade steak, are also good. Middle rib beef is a less popular cut that we usually cut into fillets and cook for a long time; it really melts in the mouth.’

Shorthorn and Highland cows on Edinvale Farm

THE POEMS OF OSSIAN: ANOTHER BRILLIANT DECEPTION

While travelling around Scotland, I've sometimes received the impression that the factor that is holding back its cuisine is the importance of the products and the fact that it is deeply rooted in tradition. This makes people wary of thinking outside the box and by-passing the rules. Perhaps a little turn of the screw is all that is needed to create a true revolution and allow the treasure that they have to shine bright. They need to turn something that perhaps is seen from outside as a burden into an opportunity.

Scottish cuisine is built upon solid foundations; it is inspired by austerity and looks inwards. Respect for tradition is an added value and mustn't be ignored, as long as it doesn't become an obstacle for progress. All of the chefs that we've spoken to acknowledge the fact that over the last few years a change has been occurring and that they are looking towards other cuisines for inspiration. Borrowing from other cultures is a constant process and the only new aspect now is the speed with which it happens, as well as the distance from which it arrives. Almost nothing now is genuine, what we call tradition today could be an innovation which was introduced just a few decades earlier. Scottish cuisine, just like others, can rely on its local products, that is one thing that is certain; but it couldn't have reached the level it's at today without the French pedigree contributed by Mary, Queen of Scots in the sixteenth century and without Celtic tradition, Viking influences and Asian spices.

Scotland is receiving more and more tourists each year. Craig and Sam, the chef and manager at Boath House, in Nairn, confirm this fact when I visit the hotel, 'Last year there was a record number of tourists and in places like the Isle of Skye people had to camp out in the streets because there weren't enough beds in the hotels'. Tourism is a great attraction and has to be so because it guarantees financial stability to businesses linked with cuisine, amongst other things. Could tourism bring an end to tradition? I ask them while asking myself at the same time, as I'm from a coast that has received many tourists for decades, 'No, there's no danger, Scottish history is very strong,' says Craig with conviction.

On their arrival in Nairn, according to Boswell's account, the travellers had breakfast in a miserable place where a girl was spinning wool with a wheel and singing in Gaelic. Reacting to the verse sung by the girl, Johnson says to Boswell, 'I'll warrant you [...] it is of the songs of Ossian.'[12] Boswell is sure that he has heard the verse before. Johnson's comment referred to 'The Poems of Ossian', which were written by James Macpherson and published from 1760. Macpherson said that this book contained English translations of Gaelic songs and poems that he'd collected on his travels through the Highlands and it had attained international fame. Some people believe that the underlying reason for Johnson's trip to Scotland was to collect information to unmask Macpherson, because the English doctor was convinced that Macpherson hadn't really compiled the poems, as he claimed, but written them himself.

12 Boswell, J. (1807, p. 105). *The Journal of a Tour to the Hebrides*. London: T. Cadwell and W. Davies.

‘WHILE TRAVELLING AROUND SCOTLAND, I’VE SOMETIMES RECEIVED THE IMPRESSION THAT THE FACTOR THAT IS HOLDING BACK ITS CUISINE IS THE IMPORTANCE OF THE PRODUCTS AND THE FACT THAT IT IS DEEPLY ROOTED IN TRADITION. THIS MAKES PEOPLE WARY OF THINKING OUTSIDE THE BOX AND BY-PASSING THE RULES.’

—JOSEP ROCA

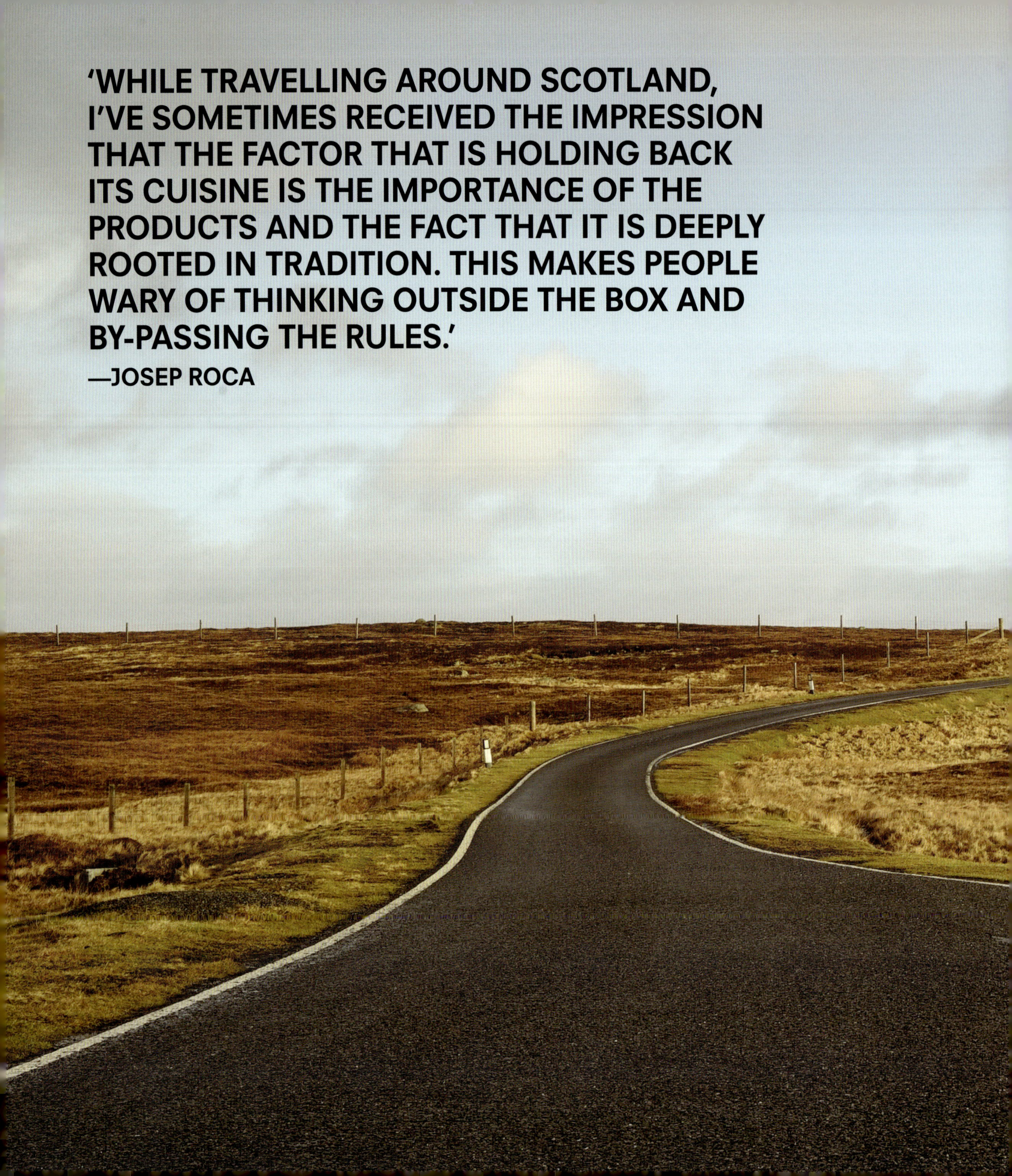

Crossing moorland on the Shetland Islands

Johnson's suspicions were partially proved in the nineteenth century: Macpherson was an ingenious literary manipulator. This was another instance of deceit, and in fact, a double deceit because Macpherson created a mythical and successful collection of poems and said that they came from ancient sources, claiming to all the critics that he had a manuscript that proved the antiquity of the works. However, he never revealed this manuscript. Why then would Johnson want to uncover Macpherson's hoax? On the one hand, he had a lexicographer's intellectual curiosity and a degree of prejudice towards the Scottish people and the Gaelic language. Also, perhaps there was his national pride: admitting that the manuscript existed was paramount to accepting that the Scottish people had written an epic whose success challenged the fame of the great classic epics. Furthermore, this was in Gaelic, a language that he believed to be a recently invented tongue used only by coarse people.

BURNS SUPPER: CULINARY LYRICISM IN A SECULAR CELEBRATION

Inverness is the eastern gate to the Highlands, Johnson and Boswell had to pass through it to reach their destination and it marked an end to any luxury travelling. As Johnson, who was fearful of the journey to come, described, it was 'a country upon which perhaps no wheel has ever rolled.'[13] The city is at the northern end of Loch Ness, which is perhaps the most well-known lake in Scotland as well as the deepest, 'Its water is remarkably clear and pleasant, and is imagined by the natives to be medicinal. We were told, that it is in some places a hundred and forty fathoms deep, a profundity scarcely credible, and which probably those that relate it have never sounded. Its fish are salmon, trout, and pike.'[14] The writers make no mention of the monster. The depth that they were told by the local people was fairly close to recent measurements: 230 metres.

At this point, Josep loses all trace of the two writers' route, as, before setting off for the most northerly islands, he stays on the outskirts of this capital of the north to visit a creamery and one of the most renowned haggis producers. In Dingwall, on the shores of Cromarty Firth, he finds the award-winning George Cockburn & Son, which has turned haggis, often seen as a way to use up offal, into a gourmet product made with high-quality raw materials.

Fraser MacGregor shows Josep how to prepare the shop's original recipe, which came from a man called Jockie Macallan who he worked with for years. However, he guards the secret that gives the product its distinctive qualities: the precise

13 Johnson, S. (1984, p. 52). *A Journey to the Western Islands of Scotland*. London: Penguin Classics.

14 Ibid., p. 53.

mixture of spices. Josep is surprised about the amount of fat it contains, 'It adds to the taste and smoothness,' answers Fraser. The rest is lamb shoulder meat, heart and lung, and ground oats. The entire process takes between 18 and 20 hours. Although it used to be made with lamb's stomach, nowadays the most traditional haggises are stuffed in cow's stomach, 'They stopped using lambs' stomachs because they are much smaller and not as resistant. Ox or cow stomachs allow you to make bigger haggises and they don't break open so easily when cooked,' clarifies Fraser. However, generally, it is most common to use a synthetic casing and sausage format. Those that are made with natural casings are made to order, for special celebrations or for Burns Supper, a secular celebration that takes place on 25th January every year and pays tribute to Robert Burns, the national poet of Scotland.

Some hae meat and canna eat,
And some wad eat that want it,
But we hae meat ane we can eat,
Sae let the Lord be thanket.

It is impossible to question the value a nation places on its cuisine when the star of the procession on one of the most important evenings of the year is a haggis on a silver platter. You also can't fault the Scots' sense of humour. Accompanied by the sound of the bagpipes, the guests stand to receive the host, who leads the procession with the food; then comes their assistant, who follows with the whisky for the toast. Before starting the dinner, Burns' 1786 'Ode to a Haggis' is read out. Lastly, the guests take their seats to eat. Traditionally, this includes a starter, such as a cock-a-leekie soup;[15] the main

---

15 A soup made with chicken and vegetables (leek, carrots and bay leaf), prunes and oats.

meal of haggis, neeps and tatties;[16] the pudding, which is almost always clootie dumpling[17] or tipsy laird;[18] and lastly, the cheeses.

Cheese also plays a part in this night dedicated to the poet, 'We send a lot of cheeses to London, particularly for Burns Suppers.' This is Callum Clark and his wife Jill, who run Connage Highland Dairy along with Callum's brother and his brother's wife. This farm has 150 cows that are fed on clover and provide milk to produce half a dozen varieties of cheese. It is located in Ardersier, next to Inverness and the whole production is organic.

Their signature cheese is Connage Dunlop, a type of cheddar that is a bit lighter, whose recipe comes from the seventeenth century and that they uncovered in the town of the same name near to Glasgow. From this cheese base, which usually matures for between five and seven months, they also produce a smoked variety and another with whisky. Small quantities of this spirit are added to the mixture to give it flavour. The smoked variety is first matured for four months and then smoked in the wood smoke from whisky barrels. Some of the smoked Dunlop production is exported to France.

After providing all of this information about her cheeses, Jill, who has prepared a tasting session for Josep, asks his sommelier opinion about what the best wines would be to accompany them, 'The tannins of red wines don't usually combine well with the saltiness and acidity of the cheeses,' he warns. 'I prefer white wines made from grape varieties like Sauvignon Blanc and Riesling. And perhaps dry wines from Jerez, for the smoked cheeses.'

---

16 The traditional accompaniments for haggis, with turnips and potatoes.

17 A pudding made with spices and dried fruits. It is steamed while wrapped in a cloth, which is where the name comes from (*clootie* means cloth in Gaelic).

18 A pudding served in a glass in which layers of whisky-soaked sponge and strawberry jam are mixed. It is finished with custard, whipped cream and almonds.

Haggis by George Cockburn & Son

THE SHETLAND ISLANDS AND UP HELLY AA

We have a certain tendency to idealise the past. The fear of loss and forgetting makes us protect what we consider to be our own from external threats, which don't always materialise. Common expressions, no matter what kind they are, help us to create an identity. This is a wealth, a heritage that we preserve as a society and pass on to future generations. Architecture, customs, language and everything that has been written using it, cuisine, and celebrations form the landscape of a culture.

As curious researchers into a culture that is a world away from our own, these expressions provide us with an easy access to this culture and a way of understanding it. It is probably a romantic idea to want to understand a group of people as one, as if everyone were the same. From experience, we know that we communicate with individuals and not with the identity that supposedly represents them; however, we can't help but look for characteristic features.

Doubtlessly attracted by a similar aim, I have come to the Shetland Islands, at the northern tip of Scotland. Here, in late January, they celebrate a festival to commemorate the Viking influence on the islands. I'm going to the largest celebration, in Lerwick, but they are also celebrated in many other rural areas on the islands. Up Helly Aa is a large, popular celebration with Viking re-enactments and costumes, and processions with burning torches that culminate in the burning of a boat. The celebration started not so long ago, however,

and it doesn't seem to have much to do with a tribute to Scandinavian people. In the mid-nineteenth century, a group of intellectuals came up with the previous celebration that took place at Christmas time. Today it is a renowned event that brings together hundreds of participants dressed as Vikings.

'Apart from the use of fish, I don't consider there to be a direct inheritance of Viking culture in Scottish cuisine. They fished in the same way as us, there's not much distance between us and we both share the same sea. Bergen is 290 kilometres away, which is the same distance between the islands and Aberdeen, on mainland Scotland.' Marian Armitage, who is speaking, is a Shetlander who has dedicated her career to teaching cookery. In 2014, she published *Shetland Food and Cooking*, a study about local cooking. 'The idea behind the book is to relay information. Some of the recipes are very common; this is household cooking.'

Marian welcomes Josep into the house that used to belong to her parents, on the south coast of the island, near the lighthouse at Sumburgh Head. The sea that they can see from the living room, through large windows, is a transit area for ships: those that travel on to America are enormous; others are small fishing boats that set sail when the sea is calm to collect lobsters and king crabs. In Shetland they've never stopped looking out to sea, 'The fishing industry is huge, it contributes £300 million to the islands' economy. The main catch is oily fish, although those that give higher returns are hake, and especially monkfish,' she says.

Marian takes down her aunt's 1948 recipe book and shows it to Josep, 'The only vegetables that are available are cabbages, swedes, potato and rhubarb.' How could this limited number of options not affect the culinary culture?

Josep with Marian Armitage on the Shetland Islands

‘Nowadays, many people grow their own vegetables at home; each family has their own small greenhouse.’ Marian talks with evident knowledge and enthusiasm when speaking about cuisine, ‘We have our own recipes, like crappit heid: a mixture of fish liver and oats which is then used to stuff a fish head before it is stewed.’ Another is puddeens, ‘lamb stomachs stuffed with breadcrumbs, spices, meat cuttings, fat and dried fruit’.

Perhaps, however, the recipe that most catches Josep’s eye, because he hasn’t heard of it before, is reestit mutton, a preserved piece of lamb which looks like a stone because it is so hard. ‘It is served with potatoes when you welcome people into your home for New Year. It’s dry and pungent, hard and salty and needs to be soaked with several changes of water, but when it is cooked you get a delicious stock,’ explains Marian with a home-made piece in her arms that a friend has given her. In fact, it is usual practice for it to be prepared in the attics of people’s homes — amongst the beams, *reest* in Gaelic, where the name comes from — the pieces are well-aired and then smoked over a peat fire, the most commonly used fuel.

Stepping away from the route physically allows you to observe the path, take a fresh breath of air and to gain perspective. It is interesting to look at Scotland from the north, when it is usually contemplated from the south. Josep travelled to the Shetland Islands to see the flames of Up Helly Aa, but at the sight of these islands located between two worlds he has perhaps found that the only common identity is fish, because northern Scotland and western Scandinavia shared a sea long before the Celts, Romans and Vikings appeared. And fish is an identity that is difficult to romanticise.

Up Helly Aa festival

WHISKY PUDDING

Serves 8

COMPOSITION

—Candied egg yolk and whisky cream
—Whipped cream
—Orange

FOR THE CANDIED EGG YOLK AND WHISKY CREAM

100 g egg yolks
100 g sugar
20 g The Macallan Double Cask 12 Years Old whisky

Briskly whisk the ingredients together in a bowl. Transfer the mixture to a saucepan over the heat and cook while stirring constantly until it acquires a creamy consistency. Cool quickly in an ice bath and fill a piping bag. Set aside.

FOR THE WHIPPED CREAM

200 g cream (40% fat)

Whip the cream with a whisk.

FOR THE ORANGE CAKE

150 g unsalted butter, softened
650 g sugar
5 g grated orange zest
300 g eggs
300 g plain flour
50 g cornflour

In a mixer with a paddle beater attachment, mix the butter with 150 g sugar and add the zest. Set the mixture aside.

Separate the eggs. Beat the egg yolks in the mixer with 200 g of the sugar and set aside.

Beat the egg whites with 300 g sugar in the mixer, then mix to a batter with the butter and yolk mixtures.

Sift the flour and cornflour and fold into the batter. When smooth, pour into a loaf tin and bake for 25 minutes at 180°C.

ASSEMBLY AND FINISHING

Peel of 1/2 an orange
Liquorice root powder
1 clove
Ground ginger
1 vanilla pod

Pipe the candied egg yolk and whisky cream into bottom of distiller receiving flask, then cover with whipped cream and finish with a slice of orange cake fitted tightly into the top of the flask.

Fill the distilling flask with an aromatic liquid comprising 100 g water, 1/2 orange peel, 0.5 g liquorice root powder, 1 clove, 0.5 g ground ginger and the vanilla pod cut into pieces. Distil the liquid to obtain a distillate aromatised with The Macallan Double Cask 12 Years Old whisky that drips onto the orange cake.

CURED MACKEREL WITH PICKLES

Serves 4

COMPOSITION

—Cured mackerel
—Mackerel and white wine sauce
—Silver mackerel sauce
—Anchovy and black olive purée
—Tomato sofrito sauce
—Garlic oil
—Parsley emulsion
—Fried capers
—Bottarga

FOR THE CURED MACKEREL

4 mackerel
500 g salt
500 g sugar

Mix the salt with the sugar. Fillet the mackerel and remove any bones. Cover the fillets with the salt and sugar mixture and leave to cure for 45 minutes. Rinse the fillets and dry well. Cut each fillet into six 5-mm-wide strips and set aside in individual portions.

FOR THE MACKEREL AND WHITE WINE SAUCE

2 mackerel
250 g water
1 ½ cloves garlic
65 g white wine
50 g extra virgin olive oil

Fillet and bone the mackerel fillets. Set aside the bones for later use. Brown the garlic in a frying pan, then remove and set aside. In the same pan, sear the mackerel fillets until golden. Add the garlic and deglaze with the wine. Reduce by half and then add the water. Cook for 20 minutes, strain and leave to cool. Separate the fat from the liquid and set aside both the fat and liquid.

100 g mackerel cooking liquid
1.5 g agar-agar
15 g mackerel fat

Bring the mackerel cooking liquid to the boil with the agar-agar, then leave to cool. Blend to a gel texture, then make an emulsion with the mackerel fat. Set aside.

FOR THE SILVER MACKEREL SAUCE

150 g mackerel bones
150 g water
0.3 g xanthan gum
0.3 g food-grade silver powder
10 g extra virgin olive oil

Heat the water to 80°C in a pan and add the bones. Cover with a lid and leave to infuse for 30 minutes. Strain and set aside.

Use a hand-held blender to blend the infusion with the xanthan gum and silver powder for a few minutes, then gradually blend in the oil to an emulsion.

FOR THE ANCHOVY AND BLACK OLIVE PURÉE

75 g salted anchovy fillets
20 g black olive paste

Combine the ingredients and purée, then press through a sieve and set side.

FOR THE TOMATO SOFRITO SAUCE

500 g ripe plum tomatoes
1 clove garlic
10 g extra virgin olive oil
Salt

Blanch and peel the tomatoes, remove the seeds and set aside for the finishing stage. Cut the flesh into small dice. Peel and chop the garlic. Brown the garlic in a pan with olive oil, then add the tomato and leave to cook slowly. Season with salt. Set aside.

CURED MACKEREL WITH PICKLES

FOR THE GARLIC OIL
150 g olive oil
4 cloves garlic

Peel and crush the garlic cloves. Mix with the oil and infuse for 2 hours. Set aside.

FOR THE PARSLEY EMULSION
100 g parsley
50 g parsley blanching water
50 g water
0.2 g xanthan gum
30 g extra virgin olive oil
Salt

Blanch the parsley and leave to cool. Blend the parsley together with 50 g water and 50 g blanching water. Strain. Thicken the liquid with the xanthan gum and blend to an emulsion with the oil. Season with salt. Set aside.

FOR THE FRIED CAPERS
100 g brined capers
1 l sunflower oil

Drain the capers and fry in the sunflower oil at 160°C until they open like flowers. Set aside.

FOR THE BOTTARGA
50 g bottarga

Cut the bottarga into 2-mm-thick slices and trim to 1 x 0.5-cm rectangles. Set aside.

ASSEMBLY AND FINISHING
Mustard shoots
Fennel shoots
Parsley shoots
Grated lemon zest
Chilli pepper

Put a tablespoon of silver mackerel sauce in the middle of a plate with a few dots of mackerel and white wine sauce on each side. Make a few dots of anchovy and black olive purée topped with a little lemon zest.

Arrange a portion of mackerel pieces in a circle around the sauce. Drizzle the mackerel with a little garlic oil and arrange a few dots of parsley emulsion and sofrito sauce over the plate. Intersperse the mackerel with three bottarga slices. Thinly slice the chilli and put three slices over the mackerel pieces. Finish with fried capers and mustard, fennel and parsley shoots.

ONION FLOWER WITH BARLEY, MALT AND GREEN WALNUTS

Serves 8

COMPOSITION
—White onion petals
—Red onion petals
—Malt extract concentrate
—Toasted onion jelly
—Stuffed roasted onion rings

FOR THE WHITE ONION PETALS
4 (250-g) white onions
8 g salt

Vacuum seal the cleaned onions in a bag with the salt at 100% vacuum. Cook in a Roner for 2 hours at 85°C. Then carefully separate each layer and cut into irregular wedges to form petals of different sizes. These will be used to make the flower. Set aside.

FOR THE RED ONION PETALS
4 (250-g) red onions
8 g salt

Vacuum seal the cleaned onions in a bag with the salt at 100% vacuum. Cook in a Roner for 2 hours at 85°C. Then carefully separate each layer and cut into irregular wedges to form petals of different sizes for the flower. Set aside.

FOR THE MALT EXTRACT CONCENTRATE
100 g malt extract
16 g still mineral water

Mix the ingredients together and set aside.

FOR THE TOASTED ONION JELLY
1 kg onions
500 g water
2 g xanthan gum
Salt

Cut the onion into julienne strips and sauté in a frying pan until golden (the volume will be reduced to about 250 g). Add the water and simmer until reduced by half. Strain, thicken with the xanthan gum and season with salt. Set aside.

FOR THE MALT CREAM
300 g milk
3 egg yolks
100 g malt extract
Salt

Combine the egg yolks and milk in a pan and cook over a low heat until the temperature reaches 85°C. Remove the pan from the heat and mix in the malt extract. Season with salt, leave to cool and set aside.

FOR THE BARLEY
200 g pearl barley
1 kg water

Soak the barley in water for 12 hours. Drain, then cook in the water over a low heat for 60 minutes. Strain and set aside.

FOR THE STUFFED ROASTED ONION RINGS
750 g onions

Roast the unpeeled onions in a wood-fired oven for 1 hour 30 minutes at a medium heat. When cooked, peel and cut into 1-cm-wide rings. Divide the smaller rings from the middle, which will be stuffed, from the larger ones, which will be used to make the stuffing. Set aside.

FOR THE SWEATED SHALLOTS
250 g shallots
30 g unsalted butter
Salt

Peel and finely chop the shallots. Sweat the shallots in a frying pan with the butter over a low heat for 15 minutes. Season with salt and set aside.

ONION FLOWER WITH BARLEY, MALT AND GREEN WALNUTS

FOR THE STUFFED ROASTED ONION RINGS

24 (1.5-cm-diameter) roasted onion rings (previously prepared)
200 g cooked barley (previously prepared)
50 g malt cream (previously prepared)
10 g sweated shallots (previously prepared)
10 g roasted onion rings (previously prepared)
20 g green walnuts

Finely chop the larger onion rings. Mix all the ingredients together in the proportions given and stuff the 24 smaller onion rings. Set aside.

ASSEMBLY AND FINISHING

Curly chives
Chervil sprigs
Fermented shallot strips

Create a flower in the centre of the plate using red and white onion petals. Stick the petals together with the toasted onion jelly so that the flower holds its shape. Arrange three stuffed onion rings around the flower and add a fermented shallot strip. Alternate three large dots of malt extract concentrate with a few small dots of the onion jelly over the plate. Finish by placing two chervil sprigs and a curly chive over the stuffed onion rings.

SALMON CHEEKS WITH PICKLED VEGETABLES AND GREEN PEPPER SAUCE

Serves 8

COMPOSITION

—Salmon head and green pepper sauce
—Salmon cheek
—Pickled pak choi
—Pickled baby spring onion
—Platillo onion
—Pickled baby leek
—Pickled broccoli and cauliflower
—Pickled baby carrot
—Chervil oil

FOR THE GREEN PEPPER JUICE

200 g green peppers

Wash the peppers. Remove the seeds and cut the flesh into irregular pieces. Purée and strain. Set aside the juice.

FOR THE SALMON HEAD AND GREEN PEPPER SAUCE

500 g salmon heads
250 g water
100 g green peppers
80 g green pepper juice (previously prepared)
4 g xanthan gum
Salt

Remove the eyes and gills from the heads and discard.

Remove the jaws, cheeks and mouth and reserve for another use.

Soak the salmon heads in an ice bath for 12 hours to purge of any blood.

In the meantime, wash the peppers, remove the seeds and dice the flesh into a mirepoix.

Remove the heads from the container and rinse. Put into a vacuum bag with the diced peppers and clean water. Vacuum seal at 100% and cook in a Roner at 85°C for 3 hours. Remove the bag from the Roner, open and filter the liquid through a fine-mesh sieve, pressing on the heads to collect as much liquid as possible. Use a hand-held blender to blend with the xantham gum until fully dissolved and the liquid thickens. Blend in the green pepper juice. Season with salt and set aside in a warm place.

FOR THE BRINE

1 kg water
100 g salt

Mix both ingredients together in a container until the salt is completely dissolved in the water. Set aside.

FOR THE SALMON OIL

200 g salmon bones
100 g salmon skin
150 g sunflower oil
Extra virgin olive oil
Salt

In a frying pan, lightly sear the salmon bones in the olive oil without colouring. Season with salt and vacuum seal in a bag with the sunflower oil and salmon skin. Cook in a Roner at 65°C for 3 hours. Leave to cool, strain the oil and set aside.

FOR THE SALMON CHEEKS

8 salmon cheeks
100 g brine (previously prepared)
100 g salmon oil (previously prepared)

Soak the salmon cheeks in the oil in a container for 4 minutes. Then remove and pat dry with kitchen paper. Combine the cheeks with the oil in a bag, vacuum seal and cook in the Roner at 50°C for 6 minutes. Open the bag, remove the cheeks and set aside in a warm place until time to serve.

FOR THE PICKLED PAK CHOI
2 stalks pak choi
20 g kombucha*

*A beverage made from sweetened black tea that is fermented through the action of a colony of bacteria and fungus similar to yeast. It has a slightly sweet and tart flavour.

Wash the pak choi stalks and pat dry with kitchen paper. Cut into triangles no larger than 3 mm in width and 2 cm in length. Put the pak choi triangles in a container and cover with the kombucha. Put the uncovered container inside a chamber vacuum sealer and apply a 100% vacuum twice in order to impregnate the pak choi with the kombucha. Remove the pak choi from the container and set aside.

FOR THE PICKLED BABY SPRING ONIONS
4 baby spring onions
20 g kombucha
250 g water
3 g salt

Wash the onions and pat dry with kitchen paper. Peel off the outer layer and remove and discard the green part.

Divide and cut the white part into 2-cm-long cylinders.

Combine the water and salt in a pan and bring to the boil. Blanch the onion cylinders until 'al dente', then refresh in an ice bath. Drain the onion cylinders, transfer to a container and cover completely with the kombucha. Put the uncovered container inside a chamber vacuum sealer and apply a 100% vacuum twice in order to impregnate with the kombucha. Remove the spring onions from the container and cut each of the cylinders in half lengthways. Set aside.

FOR THE PLATILLO ONION
2 platillo onions
250 g water
3 g salt
10 g extra virgin olive oil

Wash the unpeeled platillo onions.

Combine the water and salt in a pan and bring to the boil. Blanch the onions with their skin until cooked but 'al dente', then refresh in an ice bath. When cold, drain, peel and halve. Sear the onions on their cut side in a frying pan with the oil, allowing the edge of each of the onion layers to turn a light golden colour. Take the onions out of the pan and separate into individual layers. Set aside.

FOR THE PICKLED BABY LEEK
4 baby leeks
20 g kombucha
250 g water
3 g salt

Wash the leeks and pat dry with kitchen paper. Peel off the outer layer and remove and discard the green part.

Divide and cut the white part into 2-cm-long cylinders. Combine the water and salt in a pan and bring to the boil. Blanch the leek cylinders until 'al dente', then refresh in an ice bath. Drain and transfer to a container. Cover well with the kombucha. Put the uncovered container inside a chamber vacuum sealer and apply a 100% vacuum twice in order to impregnate with the kombucha. Remove the leeks from the container and set aside.

FOR THE PICKLED BROCCOLI AND CAULIFLOWER
8 broccoli florets
8 cauliflower florets
250 g water
3 g salt
40 g kombucha

Wash the broccoli and cauliflower. Drain off the excess water and pat dry with kitchen paper. Use a paring knife to trim the broccoli and cauliflower florets, giving them a rounded form resembling small trees. Combine the water and salt in a pan and bring to the boil. Blanch the cauliflower first, so that it does not tint the water, followed by the broccoli until 'al dente'. Refresh immediately in an ice bath. Drain and transfer the florets to a container and cover with the kombucha. Put the uncovered container inside a chamber vacuum sealer and apply a 100% vacuum twice in order to impregnate the broccoli and cauliflower florets with the kombucha. Remove from the container and set aside.

SALMON CHEEKS WITH PICKLED VEGETABLES AND GREEN PEPPER SAUCE

FOR THE PICKLED BABY CARROT
8 baby carrots
400 g water
4.5 g salt
50 g kombucha

Wash the carrots and cut off their tops. Drain and pat dry with kitchen paper. Combine the water and salt in a pan and bring to the boil. Blanch the carrots until 'al dente', then refresh in an ice bath. When cold, drain off the excess water, transfer to a container and cover completely with kombucha. Put the uncovered container inside a chamber vacuum sealer and apply a 100% vacuum twice in order to impregnate with the kombucha. Remove the carrots from the container and set aside.

FOR THE CHERVIL OIL
20 g chervil leaves
50 g extra virgin olive oil
Salt

Finely chop the chervil and season with a little salt. Combine with the oil in a container. Mix well and set aside.

ASSEMBLY AND FINISHING
Laurencia seaweed *(Laurencia sp.)*
Chilli oil

Put 2 tablespoons of salmon head and green pepper sauce in the centre of a plate. Arrange the salmon cheek and the kombucha-pickled vegetables over the sauce. Finish with a few drops of chervil oil, two laurencia seaweed tips, and a drop of chilli oil in the well made by the concave side of the platillo onion.

LACTIC

Serves 6

COMPOSITION

—Scottish cow's milk caramel
—Scottish cow's milk foam
—Milk ice cream
—Sugar cloud
—Raspberry jelly
—Milk skin

FOR THE SCOTTISH COW'S MILK CARAMEL

1 kg Scottish cow's milk
500 g sugar
1 pinch of bicarbonate of soda

Heat the milk with the sugar and leave to reduce until it turns the colour of caramel. Add the bicarbonate of soda and reduce a little more while stirring constantly. Leave to cool and set aside.

FOR THE SCOTTISH COW'S MILK FOAM

500 g Scottish cow's milk
500 g cream (35% fat)

Mix the milk with the cream and fill a siphon. Insert a gas cartridge. Refrigerate.

FOR THE MILK ICE CREAM

500 g double cream (48% fat)
500 g cream (35% fat)
500 g milk
200 g sugar
100 g invert sugar
100 g dextrose
5 g ice cream stabiliser

Mix the two creams, milk and invert sugar together in pan and bring to the boil. Gradually add the sugar, dextrose and stabiliser, and heat to 85°C to pasteurise while stirring constantly. Then blend and strain the mixture and cool quickly to 20°C. Refrigerate for 12 hours. Churn in the ice cream machine and store at -18°C.

FOR THE SUGAR CLOUD

Sugar
Powdered milk

Put the sugar in a candyfloss maker. Collect the sugar threads with a stick to form a cloud. Dust the candy floss cloud with the powdered milk.

FOR THE RASPBERRY JELLY

500 g raspberry purée
250 g sugar
5 g agar-agar

Mix the purée with the sugar and agar-agar in a pan and bring to the boil. Pour into a tray to a depth of 1 cm and leave to set in the refrigerator. Cut into 1-cm cubes. Set aside.

FOR THE MILK SKIN

1 kg whole Scottish cow's milk
Cream (35% fat)

Put the milk in a 25-cm-diameter frying pan and heat to about 60°C, removing any bubbles that may appear. A layer of cream will begin to form on the surface. The first layer will take about 15 minutes to form, with the others taking about 8 minutes. Lift the skin by the middle and very carefully remove from the pan. Lay in a tray lined with cling film and brushed with cream. Brush the skin with cream and cover with cling film. Refrigerate until ready to serve.

ASSEMBLY AND FINISHING

Ewe's milk yoghurt

Put milk caramel into a deep plate. Arrange a quenelle of milk ice cream to one side and cover with the milk foam. Top with the sugar cloud. Finally, arrange pieces of milk skin, dots of yoghurt and raspberry jelly cubes all around.

SALMON MOUTH 'GLASS EELS' AND SALMON CHEEK

Serves 8

COMPOSITION

—Salmon head sauce
—Salmon mouth 'glass eels'
—Salmon cheek

FOR THE GARLIC OIL

150 g extra virgin olive oil
30 g garlic

Peel and halve the garlic cloves. Remove the green core and slice. Combine the garlic in a pan with the oil and steep at 65°C for at least 1 hour, taking care that the garlic does not colour. Strain and set aside.

FOR THE SALMON HEAD SAUCE

500 g salmon heads
250 g water
30 g garlic oil (previously prepared)
20 g extra virgin olive oil
3 g xanthan gum
Salt

Remove the eyes and gills from the heads and discard. Remove the jaws, cheeks and mouth and reserve for another use.

Then soak the salmon heads in an ice bath for 12 hours to purge of any blood. Remove the heads and bones from the container and rinse. Put into a vacuum bag with the clean water. Vacuum seal at 100% and cook in a Roner at 85°C for 3 hours.

Remove the bag from the Roner, open and filter the liquid through a fine-mesh sieve, pressing on the heads to collect as much liquid as possible. Use a hand-held blender to blend with the xanthan gum until fully dissolved and the liquid thickens. Gradually blend in the oil to make an emulsion, and season with salt. Set aside and keep warm.

FOR THE BRINE

1 kg water
100 g salt

Mix both ingredients together in a container until the salt is completely dissolved. Set aside.

FOR THE SALMON MOUTH

20 salmon mouths
250 g brine (previously prepared)
20 g extra virgin olive oil

Soak the salmon mouths in the brine in a container for 2 minutes. Then remove the mouths and drain well. Combine the mouths in a bag with the oil and vacuum seal at 100% vacuum.

Immediately before serving, cook in a Roner at 55°C for 5 minutes. Open the bag and cut the mouths into julienne strips to imitate glass eels. Serve immediately.

SALMON MOUTH 'GLASS EELS' AND SALMON CHEEK

FOR THE SALMON MOUTH 'GLASS EELS'

160 g salmon mouths
(previously prepared)
60 g salmon head sauce
(previously prepared)
Salt

Heat the sauce in a pan, add the salmon mouth 'glass eels' and bind with the sauce. Season with salt. Keep hot until ready to serve.

FOR THE SALMON CHEEK

8 salmon cheeks
250 g brine (previously prepared)
20 g extra virgin olive oil

Soak the salmon cheeks in the brine in a container for 3 minutes. Then remove the cheeks and drain well. Combine the cheeks in a bag with the oil and vacuum seal at 100% vacuum.

Immediately before serving, cook in a Roner at 55°C for 5 minutes. Open the bag and serve immediately.

ASSEMBLY AND FINISHING

Fresh chervil leaves
Chilli threads
Freeze-dried seaweed powder

Arrange two tablespoons of salmon mouth 'glass eels' in the centre of a plate to create the impression of glass eels in pilpil sauce. Place the salmon cheek over them and garnish with chervil, chilli threads and seaweed powder.

COD WITH LEMON, SAMPHIRE AND FENNEL

Serves 8

COMPOSITION
—Brandade
—Salt cod and fennel broth
—Cod tripe confit
—Lemon purée
—Cod confit

FOR THE FENNEL WATER
70 g fennel shoots
25 g still mineral water
25 g cold blanching water

Bring water to the boil in a saucepan. Blanch the fennel shoots for about 20 seconds and quickly refresh in an ice bath. Set aside part of the blanching water and leave to cool. Combine the cold shoots with the mineral water and blanching water and blend.

Press through a fine conical sieve in order to recover as much of the fennel water as possible.

FOR THE SALT COD AND FENNEL BROTH
2 leeks
1 clove garlic
500 g salt cod bones, trimmings, skin and fins, desalted
2 potatoes
1 kg water
200 g extra virgin olive oil
80 g fennel water (previously prepared)

Clean, peel and chop the leeks and garlic. Sauté in a medium pan with a little olive oil. Add the desalted cod bones, skin, trimmings and fins, the peeled and chopped potatoes, and the fennel water. Boil for 30 minutes.

Remove and discard the bones and blend the mixture (liquid, potatoes, garlic, leeks, and cod skins, trimmings and fins). Beat to an emulsion with the oil and fennel water. Set aside and keep warm.

FOR THE BRANDADE
200 g desalted salt cod
1 clove garlic
180 g extra virgin olive oil
50 g salt cod and fennel broth (previously prepared)

Slice the garlic and sauté in a pan with the oil. Add the flaked cod and confit over a very low heat. Strain the oil and blend the cod confit with a hand-held blender, very gradually adding the strained oil to make a dense emulsion. Incorporate the broth to lighten the consistency, then set aside.

FOR THE COD TRIPE CONFIT
100 g cod tripe
1 clove garlic
30 g extra virgin olive oil
5 g ñora pepper flesh
25 g salt cod and fennel broth (previously prepared)

Soak the tripe for 12 hours in cold water. Then peel off the skin and cut the tripe into 5-mm cubes. Check the saltiness of the tripe and, if necessary, leave to soak again until the level is correct. Set aside.

Slice the garlic and combine with the oil in a pan. Cook lightly to a light golden colour. Take out the garlic and add the tripe and ñora pepper flesh. Cook for 10 minutes and add the broth. Set aside.

FOR THE SIMPLE SUGAR SYRUP
500 g water
500 g sugar

Combine the ingredients in a pan and bring to the boil. Leave to cool and set aside.

COD WITH LEMON, SAMPHIRE AND FENNEL

FOR THE LEMON PITH

500 g lemon pith
500 g water
100 g sugar

Combine the ingredients in a pan. Bring to the boil and cool. Repeat this blanching operation 4 times, then dry the pith well and set aside.

FOR THE RESTED LEMON PITH

500 g simple sugar syrup
(previously prepared)
500 g lemon pith
(previously prepared)

Mix the syrup with the blanched pith and rest for 24 hours.

FOR THE LEMON CREAM

500 g rested lemon pith
(previously prepared)
100 g lemon juice
70 g cream
25 g unsalted butter

Take the pith out of the syrup and blend in a Thermomix at 65°C for 10 minutes. Incorporate the lemon juice, cream and butter.

If necessary, lighten the consistency of the mixture with a little of the syrup from resting the pith. It should have a creamy texture. Fill a piping bag and refrigerate.

FOR THE COD CONFIT

320 g desalted salt cod loin
1 l extra virgin olive oil
2 cloves garlic
1 bay leaf

Cut the loin into 40-g portions.

Combine the oil with the garlic and bay leaf in a pan. Place the pan over a low heat and keep the temperature of the oil at 55°C. Add the cod pieces and confit for 4 minutes.

It is important to leave this step until immediately before serving. Set aside and keep warm.

ASSEMBLY AND FINISHING

Samphire tips
Fennel shoots

Put a tablespoon of brandade into a deep plate and smear into a teardrop shape. Arrange the cod tripe confit and three dots of lemon cream in the middle of the plate. Place a portion of freshly made cod confit over the tripe. Finish the dish with a few fennel shoots and samphire tips. Add the salt cod and fennel broth to the dish at the table.

FROZEN WHISKY AND CREAM ROCKS

Serves 8

FROZEN WHISKY AND CREAM ROCKS
100 g water
100 g sugar
100 g The Macallan Double Cask 12 Years Old whisky
1.5 g xanthan gum
Cream (35% fat)

Heat the water in a pan and dissolve the sugar. Take the pan off the heat and add the whisky, followed by the xanthan gum. Mix well with a hand-held blender. Transfer to a container and apply a vacuum several times in a chamber vacuum sealer to remove any bubbles from the mixture.

Drop one spoonful of the mixture at a time into a container filled with liquid nitrogen to freeze completely. Collect each frozen drop, pierce with a needle and dip repeatedly into a bowl of cream, so that the difference in temperature creates a layer of frozen cream around it. Remove the needle and set aside in the freezer at -18°C for at least 40 minutes before serving.

ASSEMBLY AND FINISHING
Icing sugar mixed with black food colouring

Sprinkle the frozen rocks with the black sugar mixture and serve.

EARTH SEA

Serves 8

COMPOSITION
—Earth ice cream
—Sea crisp

FOR THE EARTH DISTILLATE
50 g soil
80 g water

Mix the ingredients together in a container, cover with a lid and leave to infuse in the refrigerator for 12 hours.

Pour the infusion into the evaporation flask, with a 0.22-µm membrane filter positioned between the flask and the outlet towards the condenser.

Distil the earth at 30–35°C (bath temperature) for 1–2 hours and finish at 40–45°C for 30 minutes.

Vacuum seal the distillate to prevent loss of aroma. If the distillate is to be stored for several days or weeks, it should be frozen.

FOR THE EARTH ICE CREAM
500 g milk
160 g cream
50 g powdered milk
50 g sugar
6 g ice cream stabiliser
75 g Scottish fir honey
60 g earth distillate
(previously prepared)

Combine the milk, cream, powdered milk, sugar and stabiliser in a pan and heat to 85°C while stirring constantly. Cool the mixture to 4°C and add the honey and earth distillate. Refrigerate the mixture for 24 hours and churn in an ice cream maker. Store at -18°C.

FOR THE SEA CRISP
150 g unsalted butter
75 g sugar
75 g porridge*
1 egg yolk
270 g plain flour
10 g cornflour
Marine plankton powder

*Made from oatmeal with water or milk. Typically eaten for breakfast in Britain.

Put the butter in a mixer with a flat beater attachment and work until soft. Then alternate the addition of the sugar, porridge, egg yolk and flour to prevent the butter from splitting. Refrigerate the batter for a few hours.

Spread the batter in a thin layer over a silicone mat and sprinkle with the plankton. Use the side of a spoon to cut wavy lines along the length of the batter to make irregular strips, then bake at 160°C for 12 minutes. Set aside in an airtight container with silica gel.

ASSEMBLY AND FINISHING
Form a partial quenelle of ice cream, leaving a wave shape, and serve in a bowl. Stand a few strips of sea crisp in the bowl, resting against the ice cream.

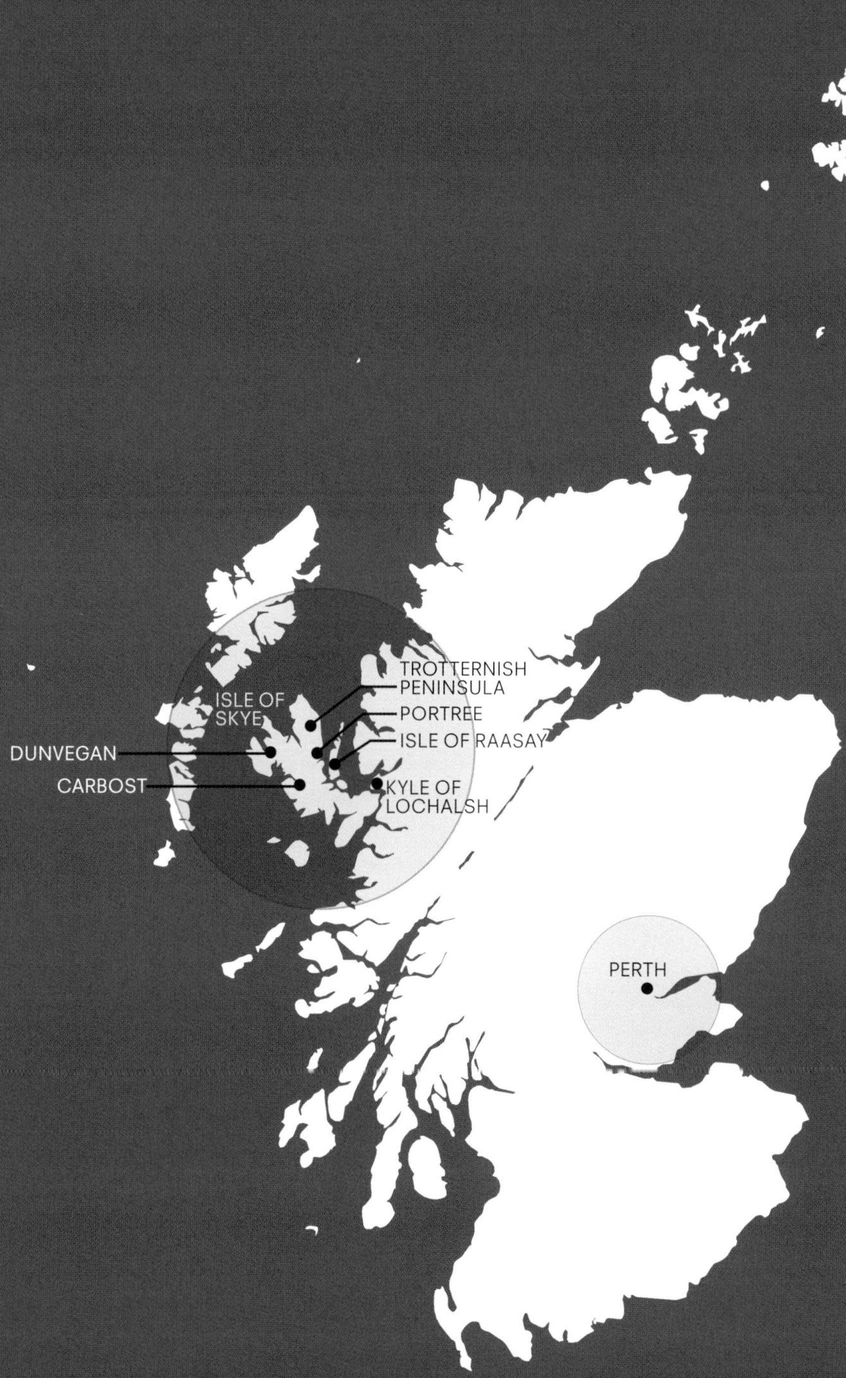

TROTTERNISH
PENINSULA
ISLE OF
SKYE
PORTREE
ISLE OF RAASAY
DUNVEGAN
CARBOST
KYLE OF
LOCHALSH
PERTH

SKYE AND PERTH

Views from Dunvegan Castle
Previous page: Ferry pier on the Isle of Raasay

Two weeks after starting their journey, Johnson and Boswell left the mainland. In Glenelg, on Scotland's west coast, after a tiring journey through a mountainous area, the travellers took the boat to Skye. The islands were the reason behind the trip, as shown by the titles of their books: either as the Hebrides, or the Western Isles, these islands were the final destination of the journey. This explains their haste to arrive and the fact that they took a month to travel around Skye.

The master of the boat they took 'spoke English,' according to Boswell. The need to mention this fact shows the extent to which, in 1773 when they arrived, the language was not widely spoken in the archipelago. The geographical isolation and the deeply ingrained tribal structure of society which was grouped into clans, although not exclusive to the islands, put as much symbolic distance between the Hebrides and Great Britain as any other exotic land thousands of miles away.

Skye didn't have a road connection with the mainland until 1995 when the Kyle of Lochalsh, the two-kilometre bridge that now joins the island to the coast, was built. The extraordinary costs incurred in its construction then turned into significant tolls for the inhabitants of Skye. Following a decade of protests, the bridge was freed from charges in 2004.

Crossing it towards Skye, you can see the jagged outline of Beinn na Caillich on the horizon. Legend tells that the Norwegian princess Saucy Mary is buried at the summit, which is 732 metres above sea level and emerges almost straight out of the sea. There above, on the mountain ridge, the icy north-east wind arriving from her birthplace combs the tomb, which is marked with a cairn.

On the other side of the bridge, to the left, are the ruins of Caisteal Maol, the castle where she lived. Between the rocks on which it was built and the Highland coast on the opposite shore, the princess ran a heavy chain that prevented all shipping vessels from passing through the sound. At least any that weren't Norwegian. The barrier was only opened upon payment of the corresponding fee. This tale was used by locals when the bridge was opened to explain, with a sense of humour, what seems to be the destiny of this stretch of sea separating them from the mainland: customs.

Jordi, Skye

The map of this island looks like pieces of shortcrust pastry that, as they've been rolled out with a rolling pin, have come away at the edges. The cracks have then been filled with sea. Some of the cliffs are just like walls, emerging straight from the sea. Walls of a rock that is dark, hard, damp and green with grasses and moss. From this viewpoint, the earth is flat and I'm at one of its edges. Seen from the sea, the whole island could be a fortress that is impossible to access. Waterfalls fall over the cliffs. I feel as though I've arrived at the exact moment that this piece of earth is emerging from the sea and the water that covered it is still pouring off.

I get tired of combing my hair back and give up. The wind is so strong and there's no place to find shelter. I don't know if it comes from the stones, the bushes or myself, but it makes a whistle that sounds like bagpipes. I would like to think that it's a welcome, that I'm being received just as Johnson and Boswell were received by Macdonald for dinner, with bagpipes and songs in Gaelic, when they arrived in Armadale in the south of the island.

I walk under the open sky towards the cliff edge. Although I haven't seen anyone since I arrived on Skye, I can't say for sure there's no one here: it feels as though I'm being accompanied. I can't make out what is under this heather-moss carpet. Every step I take, I double check where I'm stepping, and when I bring my foot down it is with fear that I might step on a sleepy fairy or elf. They have taken the place of all those who have left. The island legends are full of them. From the cliff edge I search for the mainland that I've come from, but I only find a song:

'Every island is a prison
Strongly guarded by the sea
Kings and princes, for that reason,
Prisoners are, as well as we.'

Jordi at The Oyster Shed

FACING THE SEA

In Ullinish, in western Skye, the travellers took a boat ride along the coast. Dr Johnson, from inland England, saw something he had never seen before: 'Limpets and mussels in their natural state,' encrusted into the walls of a sea cave that they access at low tide. 'In our return, we found a little boy upon the point of rock, catching with his angle, a supper for the family. We rowed up to him, and borrowed his rod, with which Mr Boswell caught a cuddy.[1]' Johnson noted the wealth of the coasts and reflected on how this natural larder could help the population: 'If it were always practicable to fish, these Islands could never be in much danger from famine; but unhappily in the winter, when other provision fails, the seas are commonly too rough for nets, or boats.'[2]

How the writer describes this landscape is significant because it reveals that fishing was a daily practice. Also, it highlights the idea that the abandoning of the sea's natural larder is a relatively recent phenomenon. There are initiatives and businesses that hint that the situation is being reversed. In Skye, the conjunction of various factors means that using the sea as a supply source makes a lot of sense: firstly, it is an island with over 600 kilometres of coastline; secondly, there is a strong fishing tradition linked to its insularity; lastly, it is a key tourist spot, and, as part of their experience, the tourists look for a cuisine that is connected to the environment.

1 Saithe (*Pollachius virens*). A fish commonly found in the north-east of England and Scotland.

2 Johnson, S. (1984). *A Journey to the Western Islands of Scotland*. London: Penguin Classics.

Although Paul McGlynn opened The Oyster Shed in 2012, the shop, where people can buy oysters and other local products, didn't come out of nowhere. Since 1981, Paul's father had been farming oysters in the crystal-clear waters of the Carbost coast. He opened the business because of the need to diversify, after an invasion of red algae in 2011 finished off most of that season's oyster harvest. This natural disaster meant that only the youngest oysters survived as the adult oysters, which filter a lot of water, died from the algae toxins. In 2017, the area still hadn't recuperated the oyster numbers they had before the epidemic.

The oysters are 'planted' when they are just the size of a fingernail and take three years to reach adulthood, when they are then harvested. During this period, minimum maintenance is required on the net structures below the water. Paul hands Jordi an empty oyster shell. It's a fair size, bigger than the palm of his hand. 'It died of natural causes, we've calculated that it was around 32 years old,' says Paul. As in the case of other bivalves, the growth rings provide a fairly reliable indication of the oyster's age. In this aspect, and in their bark-like, rough exteriors, they are similar to trees.

Although he doesn't go out to sea every day, Paul is wearing fisherman's clothing. It's a way to remind him of his roots and to meet the customers' expectations: 'They come to an oyster farm, it's what they expect to see. It's all part of the experience,' he says. Paul is clear that there is no prospect of expanding and doesn't want change, aware of the fact that it is Carbost, these waters and the possibility of plunging your hands into them that make his oysters special. And they don't leave Skye: each year, Paul chooses five of the island restaurants to take his oysters to. The rest are tasted and sold in the shop.

theoysterman.co.uk
£6.95
Mussels
Crab
Sailing
Cuillins
Boat Trip
Carbost
PIER
Sea Eagle
Slainte
Midges
The Oyster Shed
Loch Harport
Whisky
The Oyster Shed
Pier
Carbost
Fairy Pools
Sea Eagle
Cuillins
Midges
Sailing
The Misty Isle
Isle of Skye
Slainte
Oysters
Walking
Lobster
Climbing
Crab
The Oyster Shed

The Oyster Shed oysters
On the left: Paul McGlynn of The Oyster Shed

THE RECOVERED VALUE OF LOCAL PRODUCTS

There are more signs that on Skye, the economy is looking towards the sea. David Oakes has been diving the waters of Loch Sligachan for 20 years collecting scallops. At first he worked with the usual system of troughs, but with the threat of increasing sea temperatures, he turned Sconser Scallops into a sustainable business. Since then, the growth stage of these molluscs has been carried out naturally on the seabed. Once they have developed, they are taken to shallower waters, where the plankton is more compact and the fattening stage is accelerated. David gets into his diving kit and dives with a net bag every day to harvest the scallops that have been ordered. Working in this way guarantees the absolute freshness of the product.

This renewed will to highlight the value of local products, backed by philosophies that sound new but are influenced by age-old ways of working with our surroundings, has found needed support in chefs. The current appreciation of local products is a rectification for years of abandoning this link. The awareness raised by indefatigable producers, gatherers and chefs has finally seeped through. Local products have regained their added value.

A paradigmatic example of working with local products is the restaurant The Three Chimneys, on the coast, next to Dunvegan. Its menu is a eulogy to the island's ingredients and the hard work of those who produce them. This idyllic hotel-restaurant has been open since 1985, when Shirley and Eddie Spear arrived here from London. Although their initial aim was to open a welcoming, unpretentious bistro, they ended up becoming an iconic restaurant throughout the country. Since 2015, the kitchen has

‘THE MAP OF THIS ISLAND LOOKS LIKE PIECES OF SHORTCRUST PASTRY THAT, AS THEY’VE BEEN ROLLED OUT WITH A ROLLING PIN, HAVE COME AWAY AT THE EDGES. THE CRACKS HAVE THEN BEEN FILLED WITH SEA.’

—JORDI ROCA

David Oakes of Sconser Scallops

Ben Oakes of Sconser Scallops

been managed by Scott Davies, who is decided on the fact that products from Skye speak for themselves. The Sconser scallops they serve are one example, but Scott meets all his suppliers on a daily basis and has personal contact with them. This is a privilege enjoyed by so few that it allows him to do without explanations: just like the products, the menu speaks for itself.

Marcello Tully, the head chef at Kinloch Lodge, another island location serving classic Scottish cuisine, also confirms the fact that Skye is self-sufficient in supplying its products. Using a French style with some nods to his Brazilian roots, Tully also pays tribute to local products, following in the footsteps of Claire Macdonald who, with her husband, owns this hotel located in this quiet area of southern Skye.

AN OPPORTUNE APPARITION

In Boswell's book I read a text about the journey they take to Dunvegan, in which he mentions the difficulties the relief caused when moving around the island: 'It is very disagreeable riding in Sky. The way is so narrow, one only at a time can travel, so it is quite unsocial; and you cannot indulge in meditation by yourself, because you must be always attending to the steps which your horse takes.'[3] While heading towards Dunvegan Castle, the historical seat of the MacLeod clan, I think about the strawberry, cucumber and elderberry dessert I ate at The Three Chimneys. I'm so focused on these strawberries that, if I were travelling in the same circumstances as Johnson and Boswell, I'd have definitely fallen off my horse through lack of attention. I wonder about going to visit the farm in Perthshire where they're grown, although this would mean a complete detour from the route taken by the writers. But I can't make up my mind, I feel like I should stick to the plan.

Dunvegan is the only Hebridean castle that has been continuously occupied by the same family for eight centuries. The guide, who meets us at the entrance, tells us about the place and the crucial role the MacLeods played in some of the island's historical events. When we enter the first hall, I see an old man with long white hair leaning on a piece of furniture. He is gesturing and saying something, but I can't make out what he is saying. I approach him, just in case he needs help. 'The strawberries are important!'

3 Boswell, J. (1807). *The Journal of a Tour to the Hebrides*. London: T. Cadwell and W. Davies.

Dunvegan Castle

he tells me in English when I reach his side. Although I try, I can't get him to say another word, but he smiles at me in a friendly way. I return to the group, now gathered around a painting: 'It is Samuel Johnson,' the guide explains, while pointing below the painting at the extract of a letter the writer wrote to the family thanking them for their hospitality in Dunvegan during the trip. I turn to look at the man again, but he's already gone: vanished into thin air. 'The strawberries are important,' he'd told me.

For Johnson and Boswell, as for many of their contemporaries, Skye represented the convergence of the Highlands myths that had fed their imaginations. Although in clear decline when they arrived, they could still sense the prevalence of the clans' power. This was a type of tribal structure, fostered by the country's abrupt geography, allowing control to be held over the population of a glen (valley) or around a loch.

In Kingsburgh, Johnson and Boswell stayed at the house of Flora MacDonald, who has gone down in history as a Scottish heroine. Her main feat was to help Prince Charles Edward (Bonnie Prince Charlie), grandson of the deposed James II, escape after the battle of Culloden (1746) which spelled an end to the Jacobite risings. Flora dressed the prince as an Irish maid and sailed him to Skye, where he remained hidden in her house. Boswell, a Scottish man, commented on how surprising it was to see Dr Johnson, a committed English Tory, sleeping in the same bed as the Stewart Prince.

On the way to Portree, the main town on the island, Jordi takes a detour to visit one of the most photographed landscapes in Skye: the coast of the Trotternish peninsula. The changeable geology and the passing of time have shaped its basalt cliffs. Erosion and volcanic activity on the island have created

Jordi in the surrounds of Dunvegan Castle

steep walls that look like tartan, needle-like rocks, summits and arches, as if they were fallen building blocks abandoned by a giant. The Old Man of Storr stands here; a 50-metre-high rock formation, visible kilometres away from the road, that challenges gravity and the onslaught of winds.

In Portree, we find the Isle of Skye Baking Company. Barry and Liza Hawthorne are two more people who have become fascinated with the island. Originally from South Africa, they established themselves on Skye in 2007, after spending a short time in London. Although Barry had already worked as a pastry chef in their country, he lacked knowledge about the culture that had just taken them in. Despite this, they decided to start a shortbread and oatcake business as, until then, no one had done it on Skye.

Barry teaches Jordi — pastry chef to pastry chef — how to make the dough for the oatcakes. He uses two types of oats, one that is fine and another that is coarsely ground. He mixes them with warm water to activate the cereal and form a malleable dough. Barry explains that traditionally duck fat was used, but nowadays it is too expensive and has been replaced by pork fat. 'If I had a gourmet restaurant, I would use duck fat, it's more appropriate,' he says. One of the business's specialities is an oatcake with dulse seaweed[4], added as a dust to the dough. The use of this algae was common in Celtic culture as a food and a medicine. However, there is no tradition of using it to flavour oatcakes. Sometimes it's the new arrivals who, without the weight of tradition, teach the locals new versions of age-old recipes.

4 *Palmaria palmata.*

Trotternish Peninsula on the Isle of Skye

DANCING A JIG ON RAASAY

Jordi crosses from Skye to the nearby island of Raasay, just as the two travellers did in 1773. Raasay has a similar surface area to Manhattan. However, rather than 1.67 million inhabitants, there are 167. Trying to reverse the population decline is one of its inhabitants' main objectives. And Raasay House certainly plays an important role in this task. This palace, whose story runs in parallel with the island's 500 years of history, has fallen and risen again several times. The last was in 2009, following a fire, when it was just about to reopen after an expensive refurbishment. Today, it is still standing and has reopened after other challenges.

The house is the neuralgic point of the island, located beside the docking point for the ferries that come from Skye. John Macleod put up Johnson and Boswell there for a few days. The writers say that the reception they received there far exceeded their expectations and they provide details of what they ate and, above all, what they drank, in their books. While the older Johnson rested in the house, Boswell writes about climbing Dun Caan, the highest mountain on the island. The view from the summit made him so happy that he danced a jig with his walking companions.

Raasay House offers a selection of leisure activities and in high season employs almost forty people. It provides accommodation for tourists and has a restaurant and various community projects, such as the vegetable gardens and greenhouses behind the building. These supply the restaurant's fresh products as well as the island's local shops.

STRAWBERRIES AND CHOCOLATE

Dunning wasn't on the planned route, but, everything has sent me in this direction. I'm enjoying leaving the route behind. It's easier to stay in your comfort zone, but listening to and acting on instinct is exciting. Those strawberries were so good... and the man told me 'the strawberries are important'. How could I not listen to him? Just as Johnson and Boswell ended up on the Isle of Coll without meaning to, with the storm forcing them to take refuge at the nearest shelter, strawberries have brought me back to almost the start of the journey. This is shown on the map. Broadslap Fruit Farm is level with Saint Andrews, but further inland. And yes, there are still strawberries when I get there, despite the fact that the season is over in the region. The owner tells me that they plant some later on and it works because they are planted directly in the ground, unlike other farms in which they're planted higher up. This is also the reason why they are so sweet and tasty.

'I collected fruit in this spot 50 years ago when I was a child,' the farm owner tells me. The tradition of cultivating berries in this region began many years ago. The type of soil, moisture and hours of sunlight in Perthshire seem to be perfect for growing strawberries, raspberries, blackberries and brambles. 'The ground is naturally fertile, we don't use chemicals. They aren't necessary, all we need are natural fertilisers and water.' First thing in the morning there is a team of fruit pickers who pick the fruit for direct sales and shop and restaurant orders; but a special feature of Broadslap is that the customers can come and pick the fruit themselves. The farm is open to anyone who wants to come, equipped with a basket, and collect their own fruit. This is a way of relaying values within the community, getting people to take part in this valuable process, linking them with the land and what it offers.

How can you turn a remote ingredient into something that forms part of the landscape that you live in? It doesn't seem like an easy task. Perhaps Charlotte Flower wasn't thinking along these lines in 2007 when she launched her business, Charlotte Flower Chocolates. However, it seems as though she has achieved this: turning chocolate into a familiar product around Loch Tay. 'Scotland is a country of chocolate lovers. There are 83 traditional chocolate makers and, although with our love of sweet things we favour milk chocolate, there are more and more people interested in a different kind of chocolate'. Charlotte is, in fact, a forager who has found in cocoa butter and the ganaches she uses to make her chocolates, the perfect place in which to put what she forages. 'I look for seasonal flavours along the river banks, loch shores and on the hills of these beautiful surroundings,' she says. The plants she finds here are very representative of what can be found throughout Scotland. As well as her love of plants, Charlotte has a passion for cocoa. This occurred later, she confesses, through the master Pierre Marcolini, but when it arrived it took hold and was the key to a turning point in her working life.

Perhaps Charlotte sees chocolate in much the same way as everything else that she forages. Because cocoa beans are just as expressive as elderberries, mint or nettles: some of the ingredients that she uses to make her chocolates. 'We can learn a lot from cocoa beans. It's interesting to work with the variety of tastes they have according to where they come from: fruity, acidic, citrus, etc.' It is the flavours of each of her chocolates, most of which come from unique origins, that help her to identify the best mixtures: sometimes it's a herb to balance out the fat, sometimes a berry to balance out bitterness. 'When I started selling my chocolates at the markets, people were surprised. But now, years later, the customers seek what I offer: chocolates with pine, seaweed or garlic. I wouldn't make anything that I didn't like myself.'

I'm not sure if chocolate can be more than a shared passion. Feeling this passion, in any case, often transports me to the same spiritual place as the person I'm sharing it with. The calm enthusiasm and interest that Charlotte radiates when talking about what she does make me happy. With chocolate between us, words aren't necessary, communication comes easily as we have a common language. She gives me a Madagascan chocolate to taste. In this case, Charlotte hasn't added anything. However, it has the intense taste of a fresh forest. It's like something that has happened by chance, just like the fact that I'm here now.

'I'M ENJOYING LEAVING THE ROUTE BEHIND. IT'S EASIER TO STAY IN YOUR COMFORT ZONE, BUT LISTENING TO AND ACTING ON INSTINCT IS EXCITING. THOSE STRAWBERRIES WERE SO GOOD... AND THE MAN TOLD ME "THE STRAWBERRIES ARE IMPORTANT". HOW COULD I NOT LISTEN TO HIM?'

—JORDI ROCA

Jordi with Craig Mitchell of Broadslap Fruit Farm

Charlotte of Charlotte Flower Chocolates

THE MACALLAN-STEAMED OYSTER

Serves 4

COMPOSITION

—Oyster
—Oyster soup
—Pickled seaweed

FOR THE OYSTER

4 oysters

When it is time to serve, shuck the oysters, trim off the beard, and place each one in its steamer tamis.

FOR THE OYSTER SOUP

10 oysters
50 g shallots
5 g unsalted butter
35 g oyster liquor
20 g oyster sauce
625 g cream
Salt

Shuck the oysters and set aside 35 g of their liquor. Chop the shallot into fine julienne strips and sweat in a pan with the butter and a little salt over a very low heat until cooked. Add the oysters and sear on both sides to colour a little. Deglaze the pan with the oyster liquor, add the oyster sauce, leave to cook for 1 minute, and then add the cream. Simmer for 5 minutes, then remove from the heat and transfer the mixture to a Thermomix. Blend and pass through a fine-mesh conical sieve. Set aside in a bain-marie at 65°C.

FOR THE VINEGAR SYRUP

100 g water
30 g sugar
25 g rice vinegar

Mix the water with the sugar in a pan and heat to 85°C. Leave to cool, and then add the vinegar. Set aside in the refrigerator.

FOR THE PICKLED SEAWEED

10 g red kaedenori seaweed
12 g ito kanten (dried agar-agar strings)
100 g vinegar syrup (previously prepared)

Put the dried seaweed into a container with cold water and soak for 1 hour. Drain the seaweed and vacuum seal in a bag with the vinegar syrup at 100% vacuum to impregnate. Set aside in the refrigerator.

ASSEMBLY AND FINISHING

4 stones
Candied wood
The Macallan Double Cask 12 Years Old whisky

Heat the stones until red hot. Put a very hot stone at the bottom of a bowl and place a steamer tamis over it. Use tweezers to add a few pieces of picked seaweed to the tamis.

Place a piece of candied wood in a spoon and serve apart. At the table, pour a few drops of whisky over the hot stone and cover for 20 seconds to generate enough steam. Then add the oyster and cook lightly. In the meantime, serve 30 g of very hot oyster soup in a small glass.

CRANACHAN

Serves 8

COMPOSITION
—Honey and whisky jelly
—Nitro fruit
—Violet meringue
—Cream
—Whisky granita

FOR THE HONEY AND WHISKY JELLY
50 ml The Macallan Double Cask
12 Years Old whisky
75 g honey
125 g water
1 g gellan gum

Heat the water with the honey in a pan. Incorporate the gellan gum while stirring constantly until the mixture comes to the boil. Take the pan off the heat. Add the whisky, then transfer to a container, cover with a lid and refrigerate. Immediately before serving, break up the jelly.

FOR THE NITRO FRUIT
30 g raspberries
30 g blackberries

Immerse the berries in liquid nitrogen for 15 seconds. Take them out and crush with a rolling pin. Set aside in the freezer.

FOR THE VIOLET MERINGUE
100 g egg whites
100 g Azuleta*

*Sugar with the aroma, colour and flavour of violets.

Dissolve the sugar in the egg whites in a bain-marie at 50°C. Beat the egg whites in a mixer to a stiff meringue. Pipe dots over a silicone mat. Dry out in a dehydrator at 60°C overnight.

Set aside in an airtight container with silica gel.

FOR THE WHIPPED CREAM
500 g cream
1 g xanthan gum

Mix the xanthan gum with the cream and whip. Refrigerate.

(The xanthan gum ensures that the texture of the cream will remain firm for longer).

FOR THE WHISKY GRANITA
50 g whisky
100 g water
20 g sugar

Dissolve the sugar in the water and add the whisky.

Pour the mixture into a nitro bowl (or use a polystyrene container) and add liquid nitrogen. Beat with a whisk and use a small strainer to collect the granita crystals. Set aside in the freezer.

ASSEMBLY AND FINISHING
Fresh fruit: blackberries, raspberries, assorted berries
Violets

Make a layer of jelly at the bottom of a glass, and cover with layers of whipped cream, frozen and fresh fruit, and whisky granita. Decorate with meringues and violets.

OYSTER AND RHUBARB

Serves 8

COMPOSITION

—Oyster
—Diced frigate tuna
—Shallots braised in butter
—*Lyo* oyster shell
—Earl Grey tea mayonnaise
—Fermented oyster sauce
—Diced apple
—Diced rhubarb
—Green walnuts

FOR THE OYSTER

10 oysters

Use a paring knife to open the oysters. Trim off their beards and set aside for the fermented oyster sauce. Collect their liquor and reserve for another use. Cut the oysters into 5-mm cubes. Set aside in the refrigerator.

FOR THE BRINE

1 kg water
100 g salt

Completely dissolve the salt in the cold water in a container. Set aside.

FOR THE DICED FRIGATE TUNA

1 (500-g) frigate tuna
Brine (previously prepared)

Fillet the fish and remove any bones. Soak in the brine for 4 minutes. Dry and cut into 6-mm cubes. Set aside in the refrigerator.

FOR THE SHALLOTS BRAISED IN BUTTER

500 g shallots
250 g unsalted butter

Cut the shallots into 1-cm dice and braise in the butter in a pan for 30 minutes, only lightly colouring.

FOR THE OYSTER SAUCE

220 g shallots
125 g unsalted butter
1.25 kg oysters (net weight without shells)
500 g oyster liquor (previously set aside)

Cut the shallots into julienne strips and sweat in a pan with the butter until soft. Add the oysters and liquor and cook for 10 minutes. Blend and strain. Set aside.

FOR THE *LYO* OYSTER SHELL

500 g oyster sauce (previously prepared)
3 gelatine leaves
1.25 g xanthan gum

Blend the oyster sauce with the xanthan gum. Soak the gelatine leaves in an ice bath. Heat the oyster sauce mixture to 60°C and dissolve the softened gelatine. Pour the mixture into oyster shell moulds to a thickness of 4 mm and freeze. Finally, put the oyster shells into the freeze-dryer. Freeze-dry and set aside.

FOR THE EARL GREY TEA MAYONNAISE

60 g Earl Grey tea
80 g sunflower oil
30 g egg yolks
Salt

Blend the tea with the oil until very smooth. Beat the egg to an emulsion with the tea-infused oil and season with salt.

FOR THE FERMENTED OYSTER SAUCE
250 g oyster beards (previously set aside)
50 g shallots
100 g unsalted butter
250 g cream
250 g oyster liquor (previously set aside)
250 g oyster sauce*
40 g fermented shallots
20 g fish sauce**

*A viscous dark brown sauce commonly used in Chinese cuisine.

**A sauce made from fish fermented with sea salt, commonly used in South-East Asian cuisines.

Chop the shallots and cook in a pan with the butter. Add the oyster beards, cream and oyster liquor, and cook for 5 minutes. Add the rest of the ingredients and blend. Strain and set aside.

FOR THE DICED APPLE
2 Granny Smith apples

Peel and cut the apple into 5-mm dice. Set aside.

FOR THE DICED RHUBARB
2 rhubarb stalks

Peel and cut the rhubarb into 5-mm dice. Set aside.

FOR THE GREEN WALNUTS
6 green walnuts

Use a paring knife to open the walnuts and take out the flesh. Break up into small pieces and set aside.

ASSEMBLY AND FINISHING
Samphire
Sea lettuce *(Ulva lactuca)*

Mix the diced apple, diced rhubarb, green walnuts, oyster cubes, braised shallots, and diced frigate tuna in a bowl. Season and bind with the fermented oyster sauce.

Make quenelles of this tartare and arrange each one between two *lyo* oyster shells. Finish with three dots of mayonnaise, samphire and sea lettuce.

VEGETABLE BROTH WITH ROOT VEGETABLES AND SCALLOPS

Serves 8

COMPOSITION

—Thickened vegetable broth
—Jerusalem artichoke purée
—Pumpkin purée
—Fennel emulsion
—Braised platillo onions
—Scallop

FOR THE VEGETABLE BROTH

150 g Jerusalem artichoke
100 g turnip
100 g fennel bulb
100 g pumpkin
500 g water

Wash the vegetables well, then peel and dice into a mirepoix. Put into a vacuum bag with the water and vacuum seal at 100% vacuum. Cook in a Roner at 85°C for 3 hours. Then open the bag, strain the broth and cool quickly in a blast chiller.

FOR THE THICKENED VEGETABLE BROTH

500 g vegetable broth (previously prepared)
1.5 g xanthan gum
Salt

Season the broth with salt and then thicken by blending with the xanthan gum. Strain and set aside.

FOR THE JERUSALEM ARTICHOKE PURÉE

1 kg Jerusalem artichokes
100 g beurre noisette
Salt

Bake the Jerusalem artichoke in the oven for 1 hour at 160°C. Peel and purée. Press the purée through a conical sieve, then incorporate the beurre noisette and season with salt. Set aside in piping bags.

FOR THE PUMPKIN PURÉE

500 g pumpkin
30 g unsalted butter
Salt

Bake the pumpkin in the oven for 45 minutes at 170°C. Peel and purée, then season with salt and incorporate the butter. Set aside in piping bags.

FOR THE FENNEL EMULSION

100 g fennel leaves, puréed
100 g extra virgin olive oil
0.7 g xanthan gum
Salt

Mix the puréed leaves with the xanthan gum and season with salt. Process with a hand-held blender for a few minutes; then make an emulsion by adding the olive oil a little at a time. Set aside.

FOR THE BRAISED PLATILLO ONIONS

500 g platillo onions

Vacuum seal the onions in a bag and cook in a Roner at 85°C for 30 minutes (or steam in a precision oven). Leave to cool, then peel. Halve the onions.

FOR THE BLANCHED BROCCOLI

1 head broccoli

Cut the broccoli into small florets and blanch in boiling salted water for 30 seconds. Refresh in an ice bath and set aside.

FOR THE BLANCHED CAULIFLOWER

1 head cauliflower

Cut the cauliflower into small florets and blanch in boiling salted water for 30 seconds. Refresh in an ice bath and set aside.

FOR THE BLANCHED TURNIP

1 turnip

Cut the turnip into 5-mm dice and blanch in boiling water for 3 minutes. Refresh in an ice bath and set aside.

VEGETABLE BROTH WITH ROOT VEGETABLES AND SCALLOPS

FOR THE BLANCHED CHARD
1 head Swiss chard

Divide the chard into stalks and leaves. Blanch separately in boiling water for 30 seconds. Refresh in cold water. Set aside.

FOR THE BRINE
1 kg still mineral water
100 g salt

Use a hand-held blender to completely dissolve the salt in the water. Set aside.

FOR THE SCALLOP
3 king scallops
Brine (previously prepared)

Clean the scallops. Soak in the brine for 4 minutes. Drain and pat dry with kitchen paper. Vacuum seal in a bag.

Immediately before serving, cook in a Roner at 55°C for 4 minutes. Finely slice before serving.

ASSEMBLY AND FINISHING
Walnuts
Hazelnuts
Samphire
Parsley shoots
Curly chives
Carrot curls
Extra virgin olive oil
White peppercorns

Arrange 2 scallop slices in the middle of a deep plate and add 4 tablespoons of the thickened vegetable broth. Use a pipette to make a few dots of fennel emulsion, pumpkin purée and Jerusalem artichoke purée. Arrange 5 turnip dice and 2 onion halves on the plate. Scatter with 2 pieces of hazelnut and 2 pieces of walnut. Decorate with 3 broccoli and 3 cauliflower florets, curly chives and carrot curls. Finish with a few drops of oil, 2 small samphire shoots, 3 parsley shoots and freshly ground white pepper.

SCALLOP WITH CORAL SAUCE AND WILD MUSTARD

Serves 8

COMPOSITION

—Scallop
—Cauliflower heart
—Aromatised kale sauce
—Lime oil
—Wild mustard seeds
—Scallop coral sauce
—Pickled broccoli buds

FOR THE BRINE

1 kg water
100 g salt

Completely dissolve the salt in the cold water. Refrigerate.

FOR THE SCALLOP

4 king scallops
500 g brine (previously prepared)
100 g extra virgin olive oil
1 lime

Clean the scallops and set aside their coral. Put the scallops into a container with the brine and soak for 4 minutes. Then drain and pat dry with kitchen paper. Sear the scallops on the grill and cut into 1-cm cubes. Season with the oil and grated lime zest. Set aside.

FOR THE CAULIFLOWER HEART

1 head cauliflower
Extra virgin olive oil
Sempio Jang Sauce®

Wash and drain the cauliflower. Use a paring knife to separate the florets from the central stem. Reserve the florets for another use. Use a meat slicer to slice the stem as finely as possible. Season the slices with the oil and sauce. Set aside.

FOR THE PURPLE KALE JUICE

1 head purple kale

Wash, drain and purée the kale. Filter the purée through muslin and set aside the juice.

FOR THE AROMATISED KALE SAUCE

70 g purple kale juice (previously prepared)
20 g chopped lemongrass
Salt

Use a hand-held blender to lightly blend the lemongrass into the kale juice. Cover and leave to infuse for 30 minutes. Strain and season with salt. Set aside.

FOR THE LIME OIL

100 g extra virgin olive oil
2 limes

Use a Microplane® to grate the zest of both limes. Mix the grated zest with the oil and set aside.

FOR THE WILD MUSTARD SEEDS

100 g wild mustard seeds (black)
500 g water
Salt

Soak the seeds in the water in a bowl for 6 hours.

Strain and blanch 3 times starting with cold water and allowing the water to boil for 5 minutes.

After blanching the final time, strain and rinse in cold water. Season with salt and set aside.

SCALLOP WITH CORAL SAUCE AND WILD MUSTARD

FOR THE SCALLOP CORAL SAUCE

100 g scallop coral (previously set aside)
10 g olive oil
120 g water
Salt

In a frying pan, sear the scallop coral in the oil on both sides and add the water. Bring to the boil and reduce by half. Blend, strain and season with salt. Set aside.

FOR THE PICKLED BROCCOLI BUDS

1 head sparaceddu (Sicilian) broccoli
500 g water
3 g salt
200 g brine (previously prepared)

Wash and drain the broccoli, then use a paring knife to cut the florets from the central stem. Reserve the stem for another use. Combine the water and salt in a pan and bring to the boil. Blanch the broccoli florets for a few seconds in the boiling water and quickly refresh in an ice bath. Drain and pat dry with kitchen paper. Separate the florets into individual buds and combine with the brine in a container. Soak for 4 hours. Then remove from the brine and dry with kitchen paper. Set aside.

ASSEMBLY AND FINISHING

Salt flakes

Put a tablespoon of scallop coral sauce in the middle of a plate. Arrange two seared scallop cubes on the sauce. Pile fine cauliflower stem slices over the scallop. Run the flame of a chef's blow torch along the edges to lightly blacken. Add a few drops of lime oil and a few salt flakes and pickled broccoli buds to the plate. Finish with aromatised kale sauce and wild mustard seeds.

TOFFEE, COFFEE AND STOUT

Serves 8

COMPOSITION
—Coffee cream
—Stout jelly
—Toffee whipped cream
—Raisin sauce
—Brownie

FOR THE COFFEE CREAM
200 g espresso coffee
400 g cream
75 g sugar
3 g iota carrageenan

Heat the cream in a pan. In a bowl, mix the sugar with the iota and incorporate into the cream, stirring constantly until it comes to the boil. Remove the pan from the heat and add the freshly made espresso. Before the mixture sets, pour 50 g into each soup plate.

FOR THE STOUT JELLY
400 g Guinness stout
1.5 gelatine leaves

Soak the gelatine leaves in cold water to soften. Heat 50 g of stout in a saucepan and dissolve the softened gelatine. While still hot, mix with the remaining stout. Pour a very thin layer of jelly mixture over the set coffee cream in each plate.

FOR THE TOFFEE WHIPPED CREAM
200 g sugar
500 g cream
2 gelatine leaves

Cook the sugar to a caramel at 180°C and add the cream a little at a time to prevent the caramel from solidifying fully. Soak the gelatine to soften and dry on paper towels. When the toffee has dissolved completely in the cream, add the gelatine. Strain and rest in the refrigerator for 24 hours. Whip in a stand mixer and set aside in a piping bag with a star nozzle.

FOR THE RAISIN SAUCE
500 g raisins
500 g water

Combine the cold water with the raisins in a pan and bring to the boil. Remove from the heat and blend with a hand-held blender. Strain and fill piping bags. Refrigerate.

FOR THE BROWNIE
320 g eggs
420 g sugar
400 g unsalted butter
250 g dark chocolate (70% cocoa solids)
200 g flour
2 g salt

Whisk together the eggs and sugar in a bowl until thick and pale.

Melt the butter and add the chocolate. Fold the egg mixture half at a time into the chocolate until smooth. Sprinkle in the flour and incorporate. Pour the batter into a baking tin and bake at 200°C for about 10 minutes.

Freeze and cut into the desired portions.

ASSEMBLY AND FINISHING
Candied ginger

Pipe dots of whipped toffee cream and raisin sauce over the plates with the set coffee cream and stout jelly. Arrange brownie and candied ginger pieces over the entire surface.

LANGOUSTINE WITH MUGWORT AND SMOKED BUTTER AIR

Serves 4

COMPOSITION
—Langoustines
—Mugwort sauce
—Smoked butter air

FOR THE LANGOUSTINES
4 langoustines

Separate the langoustine heads from the tails. Reserve the heads for another use. Use a knife to split the tails along their length without cutting through the flesh and open the shell. Lightly sear the tails in their shells on a barbecue and set aside for finishing.

FOR THE MACERATED MUGWORT
96° neutral spirit
Water
Mugwort

Mix the ingredients together in the following proportions: 50% neutral spirit, 50% water, 5% of the weight of the combined liquids in mugwort. Macerate for 30 days.

FOR THE MUGWORT SAUCE
200 g unsalted butter
1.03 kg onions
350 g white mushrooms
250 g macerated mugwort (previously prepared)
1 kg cream (35% fat)
Salt

Cut the onion into julienne strips. Melt the butter in a pan and sweat the onions until soft, without colouring. In the meantime, cut the mushrooms into julienne strips. Add the mushrooms to the onions and leave to cook for a few minutes, then add the macerated mugwort. Leave the alcohol to evaporate off and then add the cream. Reduce the heat and simmer for about 15 minutes.

Strain and adjust the seasoning and consistency if necessary with a few cubes of butter, salt and macerated mugwort.

FOR THE SMOKED BUTTER AIR
300 g smoked butter
0.3 g lecithin

Blend both ingredients together. Put the mixture into a bubble machine and place the machine inside a container large enough to hold a large amount of bubbles. Set aside.

ASSEMBLY AND FINISHING
Grated lime zest

Put 1 1/2 tablespoons of the mugwort sauce in the middle of a plate. Heat the seared langoustine tails under the salamander grill until cooked through. Sprinkle the tails with lime zest. Pour sauce in the middle of a plate and arrange a langoustine tail over it. Cover its entire length with 1/2 tablespoon of smoked butter bubbles.

HERB AND SPICE-FLAVOURED CHOCOLATE

COMPOSITION
—Cocoa butter
—Couverture chocolate
—Fir
—Pepper
—Lemon verbena
—Rose

Melt the cocoa butter in a pan until the temperature reaches 40°C. Incorporate the herbs and spices and leave to steep for at least 48 hours.

Then melt again and strain to remove the herbs and spices. Add the aromatised cocoa butter to the melted couverture chocolate, at a proportion of 10% of the weight of the couverture. Mix well and temper.

To temper, start with the melted mixture at 48°C. Pour three-quarters over a marble work surface, keeping the remaining quarter at 48°C, and keep in motion by stirring with a palette knife until the temperature falls to 28°C. Then transfer to a bowl and incorporate the remaining quarter at 48°C, thus raising the temperature of the couverture to 31°C, ready for moulding.

Pour drops of the tempered chocolate over a PVC sheet. Lay another sheet over the top and leave to harden. Then remove the sheets, leaving small chocolate 'coins'.

TOBERMORY
ISLE OF MULL
OBAN
LOCH LOMOND

WEST COAST AND TROSSACHS NATIONAL PARK

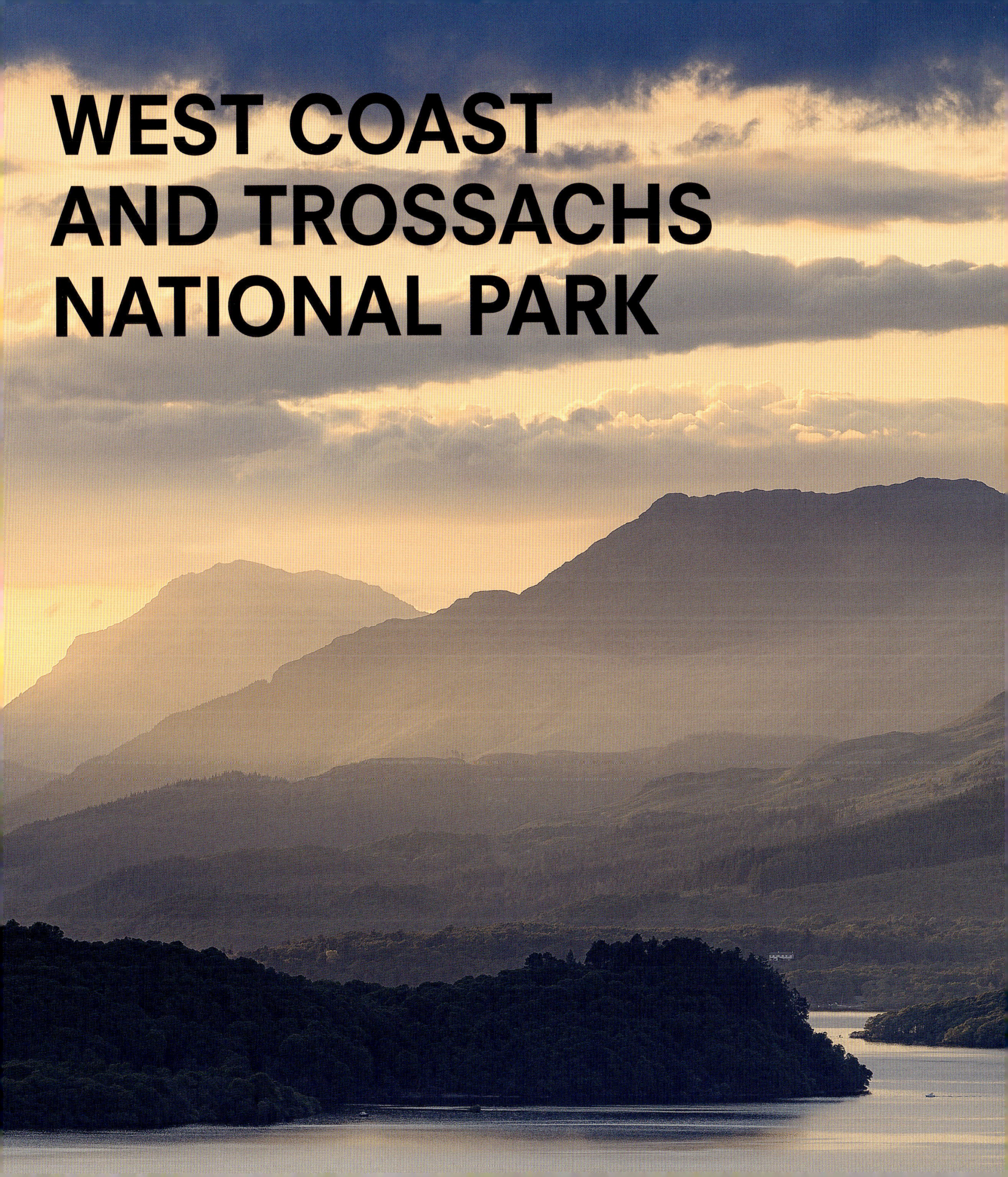

Coastal landscape of the Isle of Mull
Previous page: Trossachs National Park near Loch Lomond

'The Isle of Mull is perhaps in extent the third of the Hebrides. It is not broken by waters, nor shot into promontories, but is a solid and compact mass, of breadth nearly equal to its length.'[1] This is how Johnson described Mull when they arrived at Tobermory, in the north of the island, ten days later than planned. The travellers had witnessed first-hand the danger of navigating between the Hebrides: a violent storm on the trip from Skye to Mull nearly sunk the boat. Boswell acknowledged that his attempts to keep calm were useless, 'As we advanced, the storm grew greater, and the sea very rough.' The crew spent too long fighting against the elements, to the point that whatever decision they made, it seemed to come too late. Eventually, the sailors' experience and a change in wind direction brought them safely in to dock on the Isle of Coll, which they hadn't planned to visit. It was impossible to set sail the following days because of a succession of storms, so the writers spent ten days confined on the island, housed by the Maclean family.

Mull made an impression on the travellers. Despite the fact that they'd been travelling through the rugged landscape of the Highlands for weeks, the island seemed very inhospitable to them. Boswell would later comment on this to Johnson, '[We] have, I think, seen together the extremes of what can be seen in Britain: the wild rough island of Mull, and Blenheim Park.'[2]

---

1 Johnson, S. (1984). *A Journey to The Western Islands of Scotland*. London: Penguin Classics.

2 Johnson, S. & Boswell, J. (2006). *A Journey to the Western Islands of Scotland and the Journal of a Tour to the Hebrides*. London: Penguin Classics.

Josep, Isle of Mull

To get to Mull, I take the ferry from Oban. It's a pleasant journey of just over half an hour. A light wind is blowing, forming ripples on the surface of the sea and pushing the clouds through a grey sky. The boat parts the water cleanly in two. There are no tourists on deck, at least none that I can identify. The light in the north filters diagonally through the clouds. It's as if it were asking for permission, shy and fleeting. It is quick to withdraw, turning towards introspection. It is somehow comforting and character-building. The culture and cuisine of this country are also shaped by these beams of light that cut through the slanted atmosphere.

And what about perspective? What influence does perspective have on cuisine? Products travel from one end of the world to the other as quickly as people do. The media, social networks and chefs' willingness to show that they are inventing or using specific techniques have contributed to the dissemination of these techniques, while until recently these were secrets that were confined to the kitchen. Today, everything seems to be at our fingertips and there's an obsession with generating information, documenting and showing the world. And perspective? Perspective can't be given, it differentiates us and is the filter that makes us unique. For me it's a fascinating idea to cook the food of this latitude (60th parallel north) from a warm, Mediterranean perspective: it's like cooking the cold with heat, winter with summer, silence with noise, shadow with light, water with thirst, cliffs with the sand, the wind with the breeze, the ocean with the sea, green with golden and the north from the south.

We have mapped Scotland, plotting landscapes, products and restaurants as if they were geographical accidents. We have spoken to foragers, producers and chefs to sketch a part of these people's reality. We've set out on the trail of a literary journey while putting our pens to paper to write a culinary route. We have distilled Scotland and then filtered it.

Josep on the Oban ferry

AVOIDING WASTE: MAKING THE MOST OF THINGS

The only dairy farm on the island is found next to Tobermory and is run by the Reade family. Brendan and his wife Shelagh, the second generation of artisans, give Josep a tour of Sgriob-ruadh Farm. 'For hygienic reasons,' they suggest visiting the workshop first and then the rest of the farm. The Reades have been making cheese in this corner of Scotland since they arrived, forty years ago. The best milk for cheesemaking is that which is obtained by mixing the milk from the four cow breeds they milk: Friesian, Jersey, Ayrshire and Brown Swiss. The milk goes directly from the milking parlour to the cheese-making vats, it is then used raw, along with animal rennet for the process.

They have two main products, one is a cheddar-type cheese called Isle of Mull Cheese that is aged up to 18 months before being sold. The other is a blue cheese called Hebridean Blue, which is made following a similar process, but with added *Penicillium roqueforti* fungus. The flavours of the cheeses vary depending on the period of the year in which the milk is collected. The cows' feed isn't controlled during the months that they are put out to pasture in the fields.

Sgriob-ruadh Farm's cheeses are large and sublime. They still make them with an old press, giving the impression that the process has never changed. Tasting cheeses in a ripening room is a sensory experience that is almost redundant. By the time the product reaches your mouth, you have already received much of the information through the aromas floating in the air: the milk, moisture, acidity, cowshed, different levels of ripeness; the senses evoked in these kinds of rooms add to the characteristics of the cheese and create taste contrasts. The blue cheddar I try has an enveloping taste that is intense, with a pleasant level of acidity and ripeness and an attractive, natural blue tone.

While the cows are wintered in the cowshed, the Reades add barley residues from the neighbouring whisky distillery to the feed. This culture of making the most of resources is deeply rooted in Scotland and this is a common practice in feeding livestock. However, in recent years a new competitor for the livestock has arrived: cars. For some time, this same by-product has been used as a raw material for making biodiesel. Feeding the pigs that are also reared on the farm is another way in which they make the most of the resources: the surplus whey from the cheese-making process is added to their feed.

Brendan Read of Sgriob-ruadh Farm

'FOR ME IT'S A FASCINATING IDEA TO COOK THE FOOD OF THIS LATITUDE (60TH PARALLEL NORTH) FROM A WARM, MEDITERRANEAN PERSPECTIVE: IT'S LIKE COOKING THE COLD WITH HEAT, WINTER WITH SUMMER, SILENCE WITH NOISE, SHADOW WITH LIGHT…'

—JOSEP ROCA

Areas that have suffered shortages in the past have learned ways of making the most of what they have at hand. Whether it be due to a one-off event, a structural lack of resources or a mixture or both, in general, the Scots avoid waste. On their journey, Josep, Joan and Jordi have witnessed this on more than one occasion. Scots' dependence on this spellbinding and barren landscape was eased, firstly with industrialisation, and then the discovery of oil in the North Sea, turning Scotland into the main European extractor of this fuel, by volume. However, accustomed as they were to limited resources, by the time their economic conditions improved, the Scots had already incorporated making the most of things into their day-to-day lives.

Whisky is a good example of this: the controlled fermentation of barley grains steeped in rainwater was a way to make sure that the part of the harvest that wasn't ready on any given year, because of the weather, wasn't wasted. The other ingredients used to make this spirit are also provided by the land: the clean water that runs through the country's streams and the peat that is burned to dry the grains. Also, it is common practice to reuse the casks in which the whisky ages: they are taken apart, cleaned, polished and put back together to be reused. Therefore, it is even possible to find casks from other producers in the same distillery.

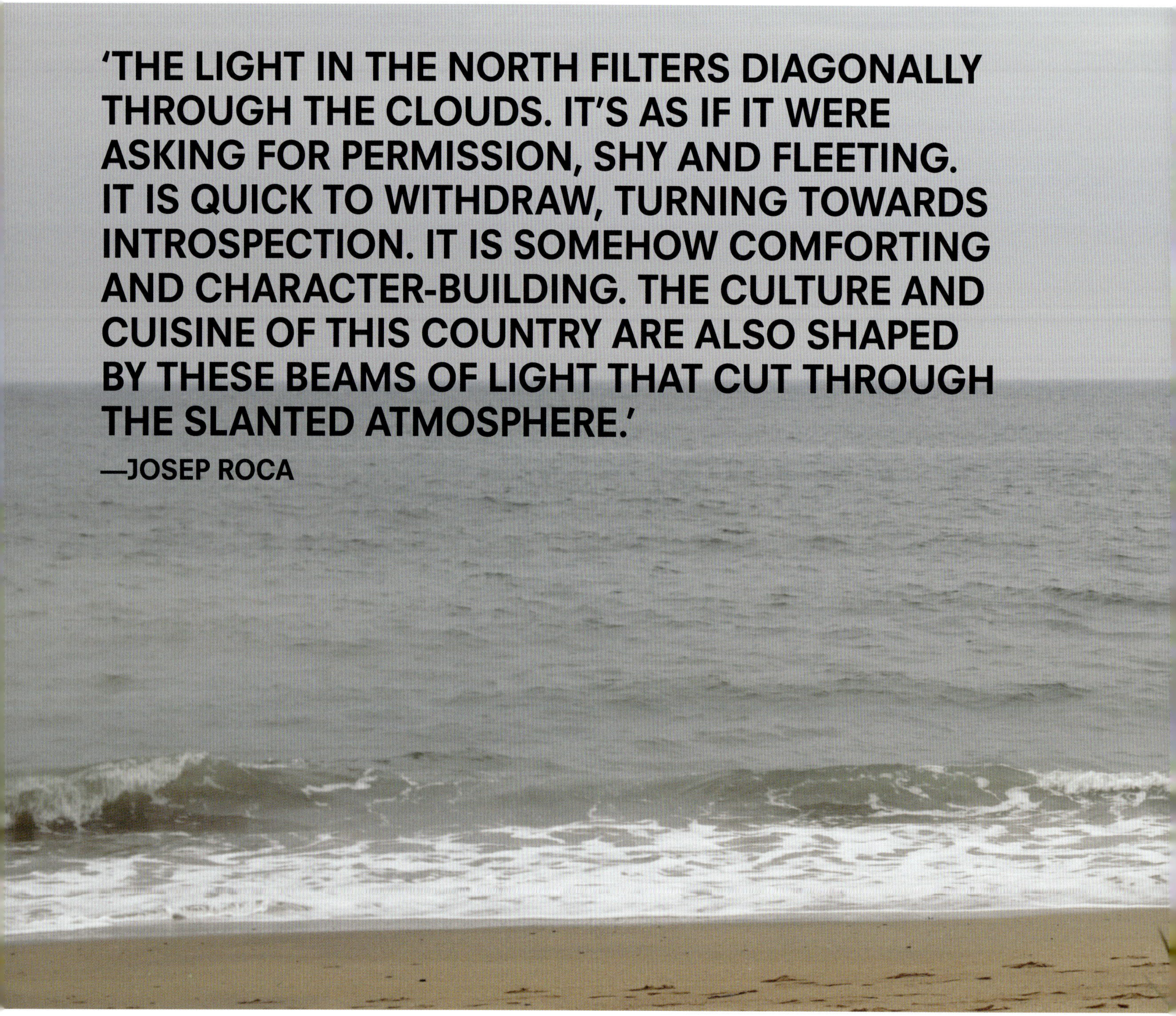

'THE LIGHT IN THE NORTH FILTERS DIAGONALLY THROUGH THE CLOUDS. IT'S AS IF IT WERE ASKING FOR PERMISSION, SHY AND FLEETING. IT IS QUICK TO WITHDRAW, TURNING TOWARDS INTROSPECTION. IT IS SOMEHOW COMFORTING AND CHARACTER-BUILDING. THE CULTURE AND CUISINE OF THIS COUNTRY ARE ALSO SHAPED BY THESE BEAMS OF LIGHT THAT CUT THROUGH THE SLANTED ATMOSPHERE.'

—JOSEP ROCA

The sea bathed by the dim and cold northern light

TREASURES IN THE WIDE OUTDOORS

Tobermory is the capital of Mull, but barely has a thousand inhabitants. Some three thousand people live on the whole island. To provide a reference to Spain, its population density is less than half that of the province of Soria (Castile and León).

Accustomed to the overcrowded Mediterranean coast, the feeling of bareness and isolation is clear; to me it's almost like living in the wilderness. The roads, hardly perceptible, are narrow and snake towards the horizon, disappearing towards this line between the gorse and the sky. Tobermory port is a row of houses, with brightly-painted façades, which was built in this sheltered bay in the late eighteenth century. The rest of the town perches between woods on the hill that creates the natural port and provides the town with protection.

The charm of this place comes from the peace, the silence and the connection with a nature that is almost wild. It is surprising to find a place like Cafe Fish at this edge of the world, in the middle of nowhere. What they do in this restaurant, found at the end of the dock, is an example of the potential of Scottish cuisine over the next few years. As called for by the location and hinted at by the name of the restaurant, at Cafe Fish they mainly serve fish and shellfish. We taste some delicious chargrilled oysters, some scallops, red sea bream, haddock and squat lobsters, a small tasty breed of langoustine with a faintly sweet flavour. The restaurant has its own fishing boat and receives daily catches from other local fishermen. What can be found on the menu depends on what arrives in the port. It is served simply and in an informal way. There is a limited choice of smoked fish on the menu compared to other Scottish restaurants. This is a fresh cuisine with some Asian influences, a fact which makes sense given the historical connection between this continent and the United Kingdom.

The bleak sea stretches out from Cafe Fish's dining room. Beneath this dark blue surface, they say there is still the shipwreck of a galleon from the Spanish Armada, full of gold, which, in 1588, fleeing the English and put off course by a storm, found refuge in Tobermory bay. Here it anchored for a couple of days to carry out repairs and restock the provisions until, in mysterious circumstances, it blew up. The divers sent by the English government in the early eighteenth century in search of the treasure found the shipwreck, but no treasure. Neither did the Scottish engineer and diver Charles Spalding have any luck. When he attempted to find it at the end of the same century, all he found was that the galleon had already sunk into the silt.

Johnson was in a bad mood as they left Tobermory. The distinguished Englishman had lost his oak walking stick that had accompanied him over the previous seven years and was out of sorts. 'He was more out of humour to-day, than he has been in the course of our tour, being fretted to find that his little horse could scarcely support his weight,'[3] described Boswell. The way seemed rough to him and he complained, while crossing the desolate landscape, of the carelessness and neglect that had caused the woods to

3 Boswell, J. (1807). *The Journal of a Tour to the Hebrides*. London: T. Cadwell and W. Davies.

Tobermory, Isle of Mull

be lost and the hills to be covered with a carpet of heather. Johnson wasn't particularly excited about visiting Iona Abbey, on the island of the same name, just off Mull's south-west point. This pilgrimage was one of the reasons they had to cross the island. Johnson had conceded to go because he knew that for Boswell there was no question of missing out on a visit to the spiritual heart of Scotland, but his indifference to the destination only worsened his mood.

Christianity spread throughout Scotland from Iona, from the year 563, when the Irish friar Saint Columba arrived on the island with the intention of converting the Scottish people. Its expansion took place so quickly that by the time Saint Columba died, in 591, a majority of the country had already converted to this newly arrived religion. Iona Abbey became a place of pilgrimage where kings and the country's great men were buried. Today there are hardly any remains of the original monastery, which was successively attacked by the Vikings. However, in its place, there is a restored building where, in the thirteenth century, a community of Benedictine monks was re-established. With ups and downs, the abbey activity was kept going until 1560 when John Knox's reform led to its decline.

RETURN TO DRY LAND: OBAN

Josep has returned to the coast that he left for his trip to Mull, this time to stay on dry land and finish the last steps needed to complete the route that has taken him and his brothers anti-clockwise around Scotland, following the footsteps of Johnson and Boswell. After making their way down through the Hebrides, the only thing left to do is to return towards the east, towards Edinburgh, the trip's starting point.

In Oban, on the lively Calmac quay, where Josep's ferry docks, you can find the establishment of a restless fisherman who hung up his fishing gear to start a new business: cooking and selling the raw materials that up until then he had been fishing.

> *The Green Shack is a 'chiringuito' (Spanish beach bar) without a beach, although it could also be called street food or take-away food. While waiting for my shellfish order, at a long wooden table for eating standing up, two 70-year-old men next to me are chatting animatedly in Scottish Gaelic. I've hardly heard it during my trip, and I've been told that only sixty thousand people, mainly living in the Hebrides and some areas of the Highlands, still use this language.*
>
> *When the shellfish arrives, I can't help but think about how intriguing it is eating it out of context. The usual association of certain foods with certain places makes me situate the cockles, langoustines, lobsters and scallops that I have before me within a luxury environment. However, here I am eating standing up,*

in a port, sharing the table with people I don't even know. This feeling isn't entirely unfamiliar: I've experienced the same thing in Galicia where it's common to find excellent products at fairs and farmers' markets. Could this be a characteristic of Celtic culture?

While Josep polishes off some juicy scallops with butter and an excellent brown crab, the owner of the business appears. John Ogden could be called a visionary. And a very brave man at that, because in 1990, opening a green shack in the midst of a port to serve fish and shellfish wasn't a common thing to do in Scotland. At this time, half of the catches that were brought ashore were exported. Almost all the highest-quality products disappeared to France, Italy or Spain. The Scots didn't value the excellent raw material from their seas, and the generational lack of knowledge about the product meant that no one knew what to do with it. This lively, outspoken man, who because of his profession was well aware of the real value of the goods arriving by boat in Oban, had to struggle against these circumstances as well as the legal problems involved in setting up his shack on the dock.

'Lobsters are overvalued; the best sea products are cockles and brown crabs,' says John with conviction. He has a perfect understanding of the product that he sells and takes pleasure in the quality of this food. He is a retired fisherman, a great fan of hunting, an extrovert and talkative salesman, 'Every year I go to Salamanca to shoot partridges. They're the best in the world, I much prefer them to Scottish grouse, which are too strong. Partridges fly higher, while grouse fly at ground level,' he says to explain his preference for the first and the strong game taste of the second. The Green Shack is just the visible part of the business that is on show, the other part, the smoke house and bivalve purification tanks are found inland on the outskirts of Oban.

The Green Shack, in Oban

Café Fish, in Tobermory

‘By law, we’re not allowed to use seawater to purify the molluscs because of the discards left by the boats, so we make our own water. We use a level of salt that is slightly higher than usual: this extra saltiness is one of the secrets behind the great taste of our molluscs,’ John confesses. Over the last twenty-five years he has gone down to the port when the boats come in to personally select the shellfish. Now, at the age of 70, he has placed his trust in someone he has taught to do the job for him, but he can’t help but visit the smoke house daily to prepare the salmon. The area of Oban was traditionally famous for fishing the abundant large salmon. There were already records of this in the travellers’ chronicles in the eighteenth century. Before smoking it, John marinates the fish fillets with salt and sugar. ‘I don’t use brine, I prefer to apply the salt and sugar in their dry forms. This means that I can choose the precise amount needed, adapting the thickness to the different parts of the fillets,’ he says, while throwing handfuls of sugar onto the fillets as if he were sowing a field. It’s not mathematical, it depends on the size and consistency of the salmons that come in; but usually they are salted for 12 hours. Then, they are cold smoked with oak wood for a further 12 hours; and the process is finished with a hot smoking, usually lasting between 40 minutes and one hour.

MORE SHEEP THAN PEOPLE

Scotland has more sheep than people. Data released by the Scottish government reveals that in 2016 there were around seven million sheep on almost fifteen thousand farms. In a country of 5.3 million people. The production of meat, textiles and dairy products revolves around this livestock. Also, the fairs and livestock auctions, with their long-standing tradition, have become another mythical element of the country. This is what has happened in Lairg (Sutherland), which, every year in mid-August, puts on Europe's biggest sheep and lamb auction.

The prevalence of sheep goes back a long way and is associated with unfortunate events for Scotland. The Highlands region was one of the areas that was most against the union between Scotland and the British crown at the start of the eighteenth century and it backed the Jacobite risings — in defence of King James II — against the house of Hanover that governed Great Britain. Its final defeat, in 1746, brought with it the Highland Clearances, a forced eviction of Scottish farmers who were not allowed to continue leasing the land. What, until that point, had been forests and arable land became large areas of pasture for livestock. These farms were less work and produced more. This was necessary because the meat from the sheep had to feed the large cities in the south, where much of the population was concentrated. The farms also had to supply the textile factories with wool.

Next page: Sheep on Bragleenmore Farm, Kilninver

Struck by the importance of these animals in the Scottish economy and its cuisine, Josep visits Bragleenmore Farm, one of the farms in the Argyll Hill Lamb co-operative that brings together farmers from this region and the isles of Mull, Islay and Coll. They all rear one sheep breed: the Blackface. As its name hints, the black hair on its face is its distinguishing characteristic. On the farm, in a beautiful spot at the head of Scammadale Glen, they are welcomed by Angus MacFadyen. 'They're hardened sheep that can climb the mountains of the area,' he explains to Josep. They feed mainly on heather. They eat wild grasses and drink clean run-off water. This feed gives the meat its taste, which is one of its most valued characteristics. Also, the uneven nature of the terrain means that they are extremely fit, making meat leaner.

THE BONNIE BANKS O' LOCH LOMOND[4]

The entrance point to the loch from where I am in the region of Argyll is beautiful. The road passes through high moorland in-between peaks, and when it meets Beinn an Lochain it drops stealthily through the valley to the shores of the loch. Loch Lomond is the biggest lake in Scotland. However, due to its great depth, Loch Ness is the largest by volume. At Cameron House, on the banks of the loch, my path crosses Johnson and Boswell's for one last time.

Commissioner Smollett put up the travellers in this centenary building, which was kept in this illustrious family until the late 1980s, when it was turned into the luxury hotel it remains today.[5] *Of the conversations that he had during their stay, almost at the end of the trip, Johnson said, 'we have had more solid talk here than at any place where we have been'. The walls of this building have seen key Scottish political and literary figures pass through and even today, it's easy to imagine the important conversations that took place in some of the rooms.*

---

4 The title of a traditional Scottish song in which a man condemned to death after the Jacobite Uprisings wants to be reunited with his lover again after his death and fondly remembers the banks of Loch Lomond.

5 On 18 December 2017 the hotel suffered an extensive fire in which tragically there was loss of life. Part of the building remains in ruins. At the moment of writing, a message on Cameron House's website indicates that they are still ascertaining when the affected parts of the building, including the restaurant, will be able to reopen.

By the time Johnson and Boswell reached Cameron House, they had been travelling the country for over two months. However, I can't help but wonder what Scotland they saw exactly. Can it be possible to feel nostalgia for something you haven't experienced? I look back on the miles we've travelled and the friends we've met. I finish the trip full of wonder at the number of open doors that have received us, the warmth and quality of the conversations we've had, the enthusiasm of the people we've met to relay knowledge about their land, how they've given us the key to the second layer of Scotland, the foundations of this hyperbolic set, carved out with nature.

In the hotel kitchen, Graeme Cheevers melts a knob of butter over a langoustine and places it under the grill. It's fundamental: seafood and dairy. Cheevers observes me with curiosity, we talk about venison, oysters, razor clams, scallops and haggis; pheasant, roots, grouse, hares and beef; whisky, lobsters, wild herbs and shoots, salmon, butter and winter. I mention cheeses, haddock, oats and red berries. In this order, as the dishes, areas, and producers come to mind. And then, he gives me the langoustine, warm and broken into halves. It is elegant and subtle; with its simplicity it has it all. The mouthful of langoustine conjures up an introspective happiness that is greater than just any happiness as it is for me alone. Graeme is still looking at me. He doesn't ask, but in his gaze I again detect the question that so many others have avoided during the trip. The locals were surprised in 1773 by the presence of the two writers. What had these illustrious gentlemen come to look for in this rough landscape so isolated from the nearby world? Johnson and Boswell sensed it: they were documenting, with the uncertainty of someone who does so while it is in the process of happening, a turning point in Scotland's history.

I don't respond to Graeme's question, I focus on the happiness caused by what I have just eaten; although perhaps he can see, as I can, that I've come to witness a turning point in Scotland's culinary history.

Holstein and Brown Swiss cows on the Isle of Mull

VARIATIONS ON THE THEME OF LAMB WITH OVEN-COOKED CONSOMMÉ

Serves 8

COMPOSITION

—Lamb stew
—Lamb breast skin
—Lamb consommé
—Lamb jus
—Lamb's foot terrine
—Red pepper sauce
—Aubergine cream
—Meatball
—Grilled onion
—Deep-fried chickpea
—Chickpea cream

FOR THE BRINE

1 kg still mineral water
100 g salt

Use a hand-held blender to completely dissolve the salt in the water. Set aside.

FOR THE MIREPOIX

1.3 kg onions
200 g carrots
175 g leeks
20 g extra virgin olive oil

Dice the vegetables into a mirepoix, put into a pan and cook in the oil over a low heat for 6 hours. Set aside.

FOR THE LAMB BREAST SKIN

½ rack suckling lamb spare ribs*
Extra virgin olive oil
Brine (previously prepared)

*While it seems logical to work with whole racks of spare ribs, in the case of this dish, one whole rack would serve about 25 people. Therefore, in order for the recipe to work correctly, a half rack is indicated (although this amount is also slightly more than needed for the number of people this recipe is calculated to serve).

Soak the ribs in the brine for 1 hour.

Vacuum seal in a bag with the oil at 100% vacuum and cook in a Roner at 65°C for 24 hours. While hot, remove the bones, fat and meat from the breast skin.

Immediately before serving, sear the breast skin on a griddle with a weight on top to keep it flat and turn it crispy. Cut the skin into 2-cm squares and serve.

FOR THE LAMB CONSOMMÉ

2 (1-kg) lamb necks
500 g water
Extra virgin olive oil
Salt

Combine the lamb necks, water and a little oil in a clay pot. Cook in a clay oven (combined wood/gas-fired) at 200°C for 1 hour, basting the necks regularly with the water. Season the liquid with salt and set aside.

FOR THE LAMB JUS

2 kg lamb bones
100 g mirepoix (previously prepared)
2.5 kg water

Put the bones in a roasting tin and roast in a very hot oven.

Remove the excess fat and put the bones into a stockpot together with the mirepoix. Deglaze caramelised juices in the roasting tin with cold water and add to the pot. Cover with cold water and cook for 3 hours. Then strain and reduce the liquid to make 250 g of lamb jus. Strain again and set aside.

FOR THE LAMB'S FOOT TERRINE

10 lamb's feet
Brine (previously prepared)

Cut off the feet at the ankle and soak in the brine for 2 hours. Blanch in boiling water three times and cool quickly each time. Use a chef's blow torch to burn off any remaining hairs.

Vacuum seal in bags and cook in a Roner at 80°C for 22 hours.

Next, bone the feet and vacuum seal again in medium 250-g capacity bags at 100% vacuum. Leave to cool in the refrigerator. The pressure of the vacuum will compact the meat and create a lamb's foot terrine.

When cold, cut into 2-cm cubes. Set aside the trimmings, which can be used to make another terrine.

FOR THE RED PEPPER REDUCTION
500 g red pepper flesh, seeds removed
30 g water
20 g salt

Cut the peppers into about 4-cm dice and mix with the salt and water. Rest for 1 hour.

Next, rinse well in cold water and drain. Put the diced peppers into a dry pan and cook over a low heat for about 2 hours until they have released all their juices. Reduce to 180 g. Leave to cool and set aside.

FOR THE RED PEPPER SAUCE
100 g lamb jus (previously prepared)
30 g red pepper reduction (previously prepared)
Salt
Cumin

Mix all the ingredients together in a pan and bring to the boil. Set aside.

FOR THE AUBERGINE CREAM
500 g aubergine
50 g unsalted butter
30 g extra virgin olive oil
40 g plain flour
10 g lemon juice
200 g milk
60 g Greek-style yoghurt

Roast the aubergines in the oven for 40 minutes at 210°C. Char the skin with a chef's blow torch. Split them open and leave to drain in a sieve for 20 minutes. Peel and purée.

Make a béchamel sauce by melting the butter with the oil in a pan. Add the flour and hot milk and blend. Mix the aubergine purée with the sauce and remaining ingredients. Blend and press through a sieve.

FOR THE FRIED BULGUR
100 g fine bulgur wheat
Sunflower oil, for deep-frying

Fry the bulgur a little at a time in the oil at 200°C. Drain on kitchen paper and set aside.

FOR THE MEATBALL
300 g lamb fillet, minced
5 g chopped chives
8 g chopped parsley
1 g cumin
1 g oregano
1 g ground cinnamon
20 g white bread
20 g water
20 g olive oil
Deep-fried bulgur (previously prepared)
Salt and pepper

Mix all the ingredients together, except the bulgur, and shape into 5-g meatballs. Roll in the bulgur and deep-fry in oil at 180°C for 5 seconds. Set aside.

FOR THE LAMB NECK
1 (1-kg) neck of lamb
Brine (previously prepared)
Extra virgin olive oil
Salt

Soak the neck for 3 hours in an ice bath to purge of any blood. Then drain and soak in the brine for 2 hours. Drain and vacuum seal in a bag with oil and salt, and cook in a Roner at 68°C for 24 hours. Bone while still hot, preserving its shape.

VARIATIONS ON THE THEME OF LAMB WITH OVEN-COOKED CONSOMMÉ

FOR THE LAMB STEW
750 g lamb neck (previously prepared)
200 g cooking liquid
(from cooking the lamb neck)
375 g chopped onion
1 kg tomatoes, peeled and seeded
100 g tomato purée
10 g chilli oil
135 g red pepper reduction
(previously prepared)
4 g cumin
10 g salt
10 g chopped garlic
50 g olive oil
2.5 g ground cinnamon
2 g oregano
2 g hot paprika
150 g water

Sauté the garlic and onion, then add the tomato purée. Dice the tomatoes and add. Cook over a low heat for 40 minutes. Add the remaining ingredients and cook for 10 more minutes until the meat falls apart. Leave to cool and set aside.

FOR THE GRILLED ONION
1 onion
Extra virgin olive oil
Salt

Halve the onion and cook on a griddle with a little oil until golden. Then cut into 3-cm x 3-mm batons. Season with a little salt and set aside.

FOR THE DEEP-FRIED CHICKPEA
50 g cooked chickpeas
Olive oil

Heat the oil to 180°C and deep-fry the chickpeas. Drain well on kitchen paper.

FOR THE CHICKPEA CREAM
250 g cooked chickpeas
15 g chickpea cooking liquid
50 g tahini
0.6 g lemon juice
3 g olive oil
Salt
1 g chopped garlic
0.5 g ground cumin

Combine the ingredients in a container and blend to make a very smooth cream. Strain, fill a piping bag and set aside.

ASSEMBLY AND FINISHING
Mint leaves

Put lamb stew in the bottom of a deep plate. Cover completely with aubergine cream and smooth. Pour lamb jus over the aubergine cream. Over the jus, arrange one fried meatball surrounded by dots of chickpea cream, one piece of lamb's foot terrine accompanied by a dot of red pepper sauce and mint leaves, and finally, two pieces of lamb breast skin. Finish with grilled onion and a deep-fried chickpea.

Serve the consommé separately.

SALMON FIN

Serves 8

COMPOSITION

—Salmon head sauce
—Salmon adipose fin
—Black garlic

FOR THE SALMON HEAD SAUCE

500 g salmon heads
250 g water
60 g extra virgin olive oil
3 g xanthan gum
Salt

Remove the eyes and gills from the heads and discard. Remove the jaws, cheeks and mouth and reserve for another use.

Then soak the salmon heads in an ice bath for 12 hours to purge of any blood. Remove the heads from the container and rinse. Put into a vacuum bag with the clean water. Vacuum seal at 100% and cook in a Roner at 85°C for 3 hours.

Remove the bag from the Roner, open and filter the liquid through a fine-mesh sieve, pressing on the heads to collect as much liquid as possible. Use a hand-held blender to blend with the xanthan gum until fully dissolved and the liquid thickens. Gradually blend in the oil to make an emulsion, and season with salt. Set aside and keep warm.

FOR THE BRINE

1 kg water
100 g salt

Mix both ingredients together in a container until the salt is completely dissolved. Set aside.

FOR THE SALMON ADIPOSE FIN

16 salmon fins
250 g brine (previously prepared)
20 g extra virgin olive oil

Soak the salmon fins in the brine in a container for 3 minutes. Then remove the fins and drain well. Combine the fins in a bag with the oil and vacuum seal at 100% vacuum.

Immediately before serving, cook in a Roner at 55°C for 5 minutes. Open the bag, remove the fins, and trim them into the shape of Mediterranean sand eels (Gymnammodytes cicerelus). Serve immediately.

FOR THE BLACK GARLIC

2 cloves black garlic

Peel the garlic cloves and cut with a paring knife into very small wedges, no larger than 1 cm. Set aside in a container with extra virgin olive oil.

ASSEMBLY AND FINISHING

Chilli oil
Fennel shoots
Salmon roe

Make a circle with 4 tablespoons of very hot salmon head sauce in the centre of a plate. Arrange 9 hot salmon fins evenly spaced over the sauce, then arrange 3 wedges of black garlic on top of 3 of them. Finish with a few drops of chilli oil, salmon roe and fennel shoots.

STILTON AND PEAR

Serves 4

COMPOSITION

—Pear and Stilton cylinder
—Caramelised pear
—Grilled pear

FOR THE PEAR SORBET

200 g water
20 g invert sugar
0.5 g juniper berries
200 g sugar
50 g dextrose
30 g atomised glucose
7.5 g sorbet stabiliser
1 kg pear purée

Combine the water with the invert sugar and juniper berries in a pan and heat. In the meantime, mix the remaining dry ingredients together. Add them to the previous mixture just before it comes to the boil and heat to 85°C. Incorporate the pear purée to the sorbet base (ratio: 1 kg purée to 500 g sorbet base). Leave to age in the refrigerator for 24 hours. Churn in the ice-cream maker and keep at -18°C.

FOR THE PEAR AND STILTON CYLINDER

Pear sorbet (previously prepared)
Stilton cheese

Use scissors to cut strips of acetate and use a scraper to cover them with a layer of cheese. Close each strip into a cylinder and fasten with adhesive tape. Cut out acetate squares with sides a little larger than the diameter of the cylinders. Cover with a layer of cheese and use one as the base for each cylinder. Fill a piping bag with the pear sorbet and fill the cylinders to the top. Cover the cylinders with the acetate squares covered with cheese and freeze. When frozen, remove the acetate and set aside in the refrigerator.

FOR THE CARAMELISED PEAR

1 pear
100 g water
100 g sugar

Make a simple syrup with the sugar and water. Peel and dice the pear. Pour syrup over the pear dice. Leave to cool and set aside in the refrigerator.

FOR THE GRILLED PEAR

1 pear

Slice the pear and cook on the grill.

ASSEMBLY AND FINISHING

Put a Stilton and pear cylinder on a plate. Accompany with a tablespoon of caramelised pear and a couple of grilled pear slices.

MUSSELS WITH OATS AND SEAWEED

Serves 8

COMPOSITION

—Cooked mussels
—Mussel escabeche
—Mussel and toasted malt sauce
—Laurencia seaweed purée
—Deep-fried oats
—Sugar-coated oats

FOR THE BRINE

1 kg water
100 g salt

Completely dissolve the salt in the cold water in a container. Set aside.

FOR THE COOKED MUSSELS

3 kg wild mussels
Brine (previously prepared)

Clean the mussel shells and immerse in the brine for 5 minutes. Rinse and drain well. Vacuum seal in a bag at 100% and cook in a Roner at 85°C for 7 minutes. Cool quickly in an ice bath. Open the bag and set aside both the mussels and their liquor collected in the bag. Open the cooked mussels and set aside both the meat and the liquor from inside the shells. Discard the shells.

FOR THE MUSSEL ESCABECHE

800 g cooked mussels (previously prepared)
200 g mussel liquor (previously prepared)
20 g garlic
60 g onion
50 g carrots
200 g extra virgin olive oil
30 g sherry vinegar
3 g dried thyme
3 g dried rosemary
1 dried bay leaf
1 g black peppercorns

Peel, wash and cut the carrot into 3-mm-thick slices. Crush the unpeeled garlic. Peel and cut the onion into julienne strips.

Brown the garlic in a pan with a little oil. Then add the carrots and onion.

Sauté for 20 minutes, then add the herbs and freshly ground pepper.

Cook for 5 more minutes and add the mussels, liquor and remaining oil. Cook over a very low heat for 2 hours and adjust the seasoning with the vinegar. Leave to cook for about 1 more hour. Cool quickly and refrigerate for 24 hours.

Heat the mixture until it comes to the boil, then blend in a Thermomix. Finally, strain, season with salt and set aside.

FOR THE TOASTED MALT INFUSION

50 g toasted malt
300 g still mineral water

Blend the ingredients together. Transfer to a pan and bring to the boil. Strain and set aside.

FOR THE MUSSEL AND TOASTED MALT SAUCE

60 g toasted malt infusion (previously prepared)
100 g mussel liquor (previously prepared)
0.3 g xanthan gum

Mix all the ingredients, then use a hand-held blender to blend until the xanthan gum has dissolved completely and the mixture thickens. Set aside.

FOR THE LAURENCIA SEAWEED PURÉE

200 g laurencia seaweed *(Laurencia sp.)*
10 g extra virgin olive oil

Sweat the seaweed in a frying pan over a low heat with the olive oil. Remove and purée lightly with a hand-held blender. Fill a piping bag and set aside.

MUSSELS WITH OATS AND SEAWEED

FOR THE COOKED OATS

100 g rolled oats
1 kg water
4 g salt

Soak the oats in 250 g of water in a container for at least 12 hours in the refrigerator. Then drain and combine the oats with the remaining water in a pan. Bring to the boil and cook for about 20 minutes. Take out the cooked oats, drain off the excess water and dry. Set aside.

FOR THE DEEP-FRIED OATS

50 g cooked oats (previously prepared)
250 g sunflower oil
Salt

Spread the cooked oats over a silicone mat, spacing apart. Dry out in a dehydrator at 55°C for about 3 hours. Heat the oil in a pan. With the oil at 210°C, deep-fry the oats until light golden. Drain on kitchen paper and season with salt. Set aside.

FOR THE SUGAR-COATED OATS

50 g cooked oats (previously prepared)
25 g sugar
15 g water
Salt

Spread the cooked oats over a silicone mat, spacing apart. Dry out in a dehydrator at 55°C for about 1 hour 30 minutes. Remove and set aside.

Mix the water with the sugar in a pan and bring to the boil. Then add the oats and leave over the heat without allowing the oats to colour. As the water evaporates, the sugar will begin to crystallise. Then remove the pan from the heat and allow the water to continue to evaporate until all the oats develop a sugar coating. Season with salt and set aside.

ASSEMBLY AND FINISHING

Velvet horn seaweed *(Codium tomentosum)*
Laurencia seaweed *(Laurencia sp.)*

Put two tablespoons of the mussel and toasted malt sauce in the middle of a plate. Arrange 5 mussels in a line over the sauce and alternate with the laurencia purée and the velvet horn seaweed. Scatter a few deep-fried oats and sugar-coated oats around the mussels. Finish the dish with a few drops of mussel escabeche and laurencia seaweed tips.

GRILLED SALMON CONSOMMÉ

FOR THE YELLOW PEPPER GEL
450 g yellow peppers (or 150 g yellow pepper purée)
0.3 g xanthan gum

Clean the peppers and purée the flesh to obtain 150 g. Thicken with the xanthan gum and remove any air. Transfer to a squeeze bottle and set aside.

FOR THE RED PEPPER GEL
450 g red peppers (or 150 g red pepper purée)
0.3 g xanthan gum

Clean the peppers and purée the flesh to obtain 150 g. Thicken with the xanthan gum and remove any air. Transfer to a squeeze bottle and set aside.

FOR THE GARLIC CREAM
50 g garlic cloves
100 g water
0.6 g xanthan gum
Salt

Peel the garlic cloves and blanch starting with cold water. Repeat the process three times. Remove the green germ from the cloves. Combine with the remaining ingredients and blend. Strain and set aside in a squeeze bottle.

ASSEMBLY AND FINISHING
Fennel shoots
Dill shoots
Chervil shoots
Chives

Pipe a line of garlic cream on one side of a plate and arrange the salmon over it. Add hot grilled salmon consommé to the plate and carefully make dots of parsley, red pepper and yellow pepper gel over it. Finish with the fennel, dill and chervil shoots and a chive tip.

GRILLED SALMON CONSOMMÉ

Serves 8

COMPOSITION
—Salmon
—Grilled salmon consommé
—Parsley gel
—Yellow pepper gel
—Red pepper gel
—Garlic cream

FOR THE BRINE
1 kg water
100 g salt

Completely dissolve the salt in the cold water. Set aside.

FOR THE SALMON
1 salmon fillet
Brine (previously prepared)
Extra virgin olive oil

Remove any bones and the skin from the fillet. Put the brine into a container and soak the fillet for 4 minutes. Drain and pat dry with kitchen paper. Cut the fillet into 70-g rectangular portions. Vacuum seal each portion in a bag with oil at 100% vacuum and cook in a Roner for 10 minutes at 50°C.

Take the fillet portions out of their bags, wipe off the excess oil with kitchen paper and set aside on plates.

FOR THE GRILLED SALMON CONSOMMÉ
250 g salmon bones
15 g extra virgin olive oil
250 g water
0.6 g xanthan gum

Pour a little oil over the salmon bones and sear on a griddle over embers until well toasted and with a good smoky aroma. Transfer to a pan with the water and heat to 85°C. Cover with an airtight lid and infuse for 15 minutes. Then filter the liquid through a fine conical sieve, and again through a fine-mesh sieve. Cool quickly in a blast chiller. Finally, blend with the xanthan gum and set aside.

FOR THE PARSLEY GEL
50 g parsley leaves
150 g water
0.48 g xanthan gum
Salt

Blanch the parsley in boiling water for 20 seconds and remove. Refresh in an ice bath, then transfer the blanching water to another container and cool. Blend the leaves and blanching water until smooth. Press through a fine conical sieve in order to recover as much of the parsley water as possible.

Blend with the xanthan gum to thicken, then season with salt and remove any air in a chamber vacuum sealer. If this is not available, rest the liquid until the air dissipates. Transfer to a squeeze bottle and set aside.

CHEDDAR AND EGG CUSTARD WITH APRICOT

Serves 8

COMPOSITION
—Cheddar and egg custard
—Warm apricot cream
—Cheddar crisp

FOR THE CHEDDAR AND EGG CUSTARD
500 g milk
300 g cheddar cheese
6 egg yolks
1 egg white
80 g sugar

Bring the milk to the boil in a pan and add the cheese in pieces. In a bowl, mix the egg yolks with the white and sugar, whisking until smooth, then add the milk and cheese mixture. Incorporate well, then pour the custard into silicone moulds and bake at 90°C for 45 minutes. Set aside in the refrigerator.

FOR THE SIMPLE SUGAR SYRUP
200 g water
200 g sugar

Combine the ingredients in a pan and bring to the boil. Leave to cool and set aside.

FOR THE WARM APRICOT CREAM
500 g apricots
150 g simple sugar syrup (previously prepared)
125 g unsalted butter

Peel and cut up the apricots. Bring the syrup to the boil in a saucepan and add the apricots. When well cooked, blend in a liquidiser while adding the butter. Set aside.

FOR THE CHEDDAR CRISP
1 sheet filo pastry
50 g unsalted butter
30 g cheddar cheese
50 g icing sugar

Cut the cheese into pieces, mix with the butter in a pan and place over the heat. When the cheese and butter melt, brush the pastry with the mixture and dust with icing sugar. Bake at 170°C for 12 minutes. Set aside in an airtight container with silica gel.

ASSEMBLY AND FINISHING
Grated cheddar cheese
Dried apricots

Put a tablespoon of the cheese custard on a dessert plate. Put a teaspoon of warm apricot cream over the custard and stand pieces of cheese crisp by inserting into the cream. Finish by grating cheese over the top and add a few pieces of dried apricot.

SPIDER CRAB WITH BRUTESCA SAUCE

Serves 8

COMPOSITION

—Spider crab
—Spider crab brutesca sauce
—Spider crab sauce

SPIDER CRAB

4 (1-kg) spider crabs
Water
Salt

Cook the crabs for 10 minutes in boiling salted water. Cool in an ice bath. Pick out the white meat from the claws and body, removing all traces of shell. Set aside the meat and the shells and carapace.

FOR THE SPIDER CRAB BRUTESCA SAUCE

4 spider crab carapaces (previously set aside)
Salt

Remove the brown meat from inside the carapaces. Optionally, the carapace can be set aside for use when serving. Blend and pass through a fine-mesh sieve. Season with salt and set aside.

FOR THE MIREPOIX

1.3 kg onions
200 g carrots
175 g leeks
20 g extra virgin olive oil

Dice the vegetables into a mirepoix, put into a pan and cook in the oil over a low heat for 6 hours. Set aside.

FOR THE SPIDER CRAB SAUCE

600 g spider crab shells (previously set aside)
50 g mirepoix (previously prepared)
Water
Olive oil

Sauté the crab shells in a pan with oil. Add the mirepoix and cover with water. Boil for 30 minutes. Strain and reduce the liquid by two-thirds. Set aside and keep warm.

ASSEMBLY AND FINISHING

Fennel shoots
Samphire
Phytoplankton

Put brutesca sauce in a deep plate, or use the crab's carapace, and arrange the white meat in the centre, topped with fennel shoots and samphire. Finally, drizzle around the brutesca sauce with the spider crab sauce and sprinkle with phytoplankton.

‘WE’VE SET OUT ON THE TRAIL OF A LITERARY JOURNEY WHILE PUTTING OUR PENS TO PAPER TO WRITE A CULINARY ROUTE. WE HAVE DISTILLED SCOTLAND AND THEN FILTERED IT.’

—JOSEP ROCA

We would like to thank:

The whole team from The Macallan, in particular Alison Tuck, Glen Gribbon, Jaume Ferras, Paul Condron, Ken & Aida Grier, Nick Savage, Polly Logan, Robert Mitchell, Sarah Burgess, Scott McCroskie and Stuart MacPherson.

The team from Master For You: Alex García Martínez, Jessica Gómez Remacho, Laura Otálora Pardo, Lydia Martínez Fliquete, Marta Bellavista Nualart.

Our travel companions in Scotland, Ben Reade & Michael Innes.

All of the people from Scotland who we encountered along the way: Andres Concordo, Andrew Radford, Angus MacFadyen, Anthony Carroll, Barry Hawthorne, Bartek Bukowski, Ben Oakes, Bill Dean, Brendan Reade, Briegot Sevum, Callum Clark, Charlotte Flower, Colin Lyall, Craig Mitchell, Craig Munro, Craig Wilson, David Littlewood, David Oakes, Douglas MacKenzie, Edward A. I. Riley, Fraser MacGregor, Garry Watson, Garth Reade, Gary Goldie, Graeme Cheevers, Graeme Clark, Guillemette Barthouil, Hamish Martin, Iain R. Spink, Irene Urquhart, Jake Swindells, James Forbes, James M. G. Grant, Jane McMinn, Jane Stewart, Jeroen Roskam, Jill Clark, Jock Gibson, John Donald, John Falconer, John Ogden, John William Gillies, Kate Smith, Katie Alexandra Francis, Katie O'Brien, Kirsty Moore, Lesley MacRacken, Linda C. Rowe, Lindsay Wilson, Liza Hawthorne, Lucy Carroll, Marcello Tully, Marian Armitage, Mark Astley Jones, Mark Smith, Martin Robson, Martine Chapman, Mathilde Halouriere, Michael James Woolcock, Neil Munro, Paul Kitching, Paul MacKay, Paul McGlynn, Roberto Jelavy, Ross Cochrane, Rupert Waites, Ryan MacKay, Sam Matheson, Sandy Pattullo, Scott Davies, Thomas Swankie, Tom Chisholm, Tom Kitchin, Wendy Seel.

Our family, Alejandra Rivas, Anna Payet, Encarnación Tirado, Marc Roca, Maria Roca, Marina Roca, Martí Roca.

Our team, in particular Berenguer Grifols, Bernat Plana, Dani Martínez, Eric Oliu, Héloïse Vilaseca, Hernán Luchetti, Joana Pedret, Nacho Baucells, Marianna Suárez, Melxor Montero, Yunju Choi.

... And to all the people who make up the El Celler de Can Roca family, without whom we would not have been able to complete this project, our sincere thanks.

RECIPE INDEX

With the support and collaboration of:

First English edition: Barcelona, November 2018
Licensing by Roca Llibres (Jorofon, S.L.), owner of the usage rights.
This edition: © Librooks Barcelona, SL
Librooks Cooking Collection – www.librooks.es

Literary counsel: Fernando Martínez-Conde
Food photography: Joan Pujol-Creus
Layout and design: Quim Gual (Blank Estudi)
Editorial manager: Cèlia Pujals
Editorial services: Librooks Barcelona, SL
Communication services: Master For You

Foreword: © Scott McCroskie, 2018
Foreword: © Isaac McHale, 2018
Photography of dishes: © Joan Pujol-Creus, 2018
Landscape photography and portraits: © Laura Otálora and Àlex García Martínez
Translation: © Cillero & de Motta

ISBN: 978-84-948725-3-2
Legal deposit: DL B 22660-2018
Printing and binding: Finidr, s.r.o.